Excelsior Publishing House

Lessons in Horse Judging

An Illustrated Practical Guide for Dealers and Buyers

Excelsior Publishing House

Lessons in Horse Judging
An Illustrated Practical Guide for Dealers and Buyers

ISBN/EAN: 9783337067649

Printed in Europe, USA, Canada, Australia, Japan

Cover: Foto ©Andreas Hilbeck / pixelio.de

More available books at **www.hansebooks.com**

PREFACE.

THE author has endeavored in the following pages to place on a rational basis a subject that has hitherto been taught dogmatically, if indeed it can be truly said to have ever been taught at all.

The vast wealth in horse flesh, so materially affected by selection of breeding stock, that is invested in the civilized world, is the author's excuse for bringing out this little work.

In the case of the domesticated animals man's protective interference entirely puts aside the great natural law, the survival of the fittest, which obtains with such salutary effects among non-domesticated animals. Were all the horses of the civilized world gathered into a field, and this field placed side by side with one containing all the antelopes of South Africa, the great law we have mentioned would be most strikingly demonstrated; one field would exhibit the perfect, the halt and the blind, a medley of beauty, and wretched deformity; whilst the other would show only grace, elegance and excess of life.

At present the breeding of racing stock only approaches the great law of survival of the fittest, much care being taken to register results, and the representatives of best results are set apart to reproduce their like. A more perfect combination of scientific and logical method than is followed in the reproduction of racing stock does not obtain in any physicist's laboratory. With no other class of horse is this method applicable; hence the necessity of judging by other and less exact methods, and therefore the necessity of some such way as has been indicated.

Lastly, it is desirable here to point out that the book is not written with any intention of standing in place of the *thinking out* process of the learner, but is more as a guide *to* the lines along which thought must be directed. By using it as a guide, and *thinking out* the subject for himself, the author believes that any one of intelligence may in a very few months, by observation and diligence, become a scientific judge of a horse.

The author craves indulgence, as the work is entirely original.

London, March, 1879.

CONTENTS.

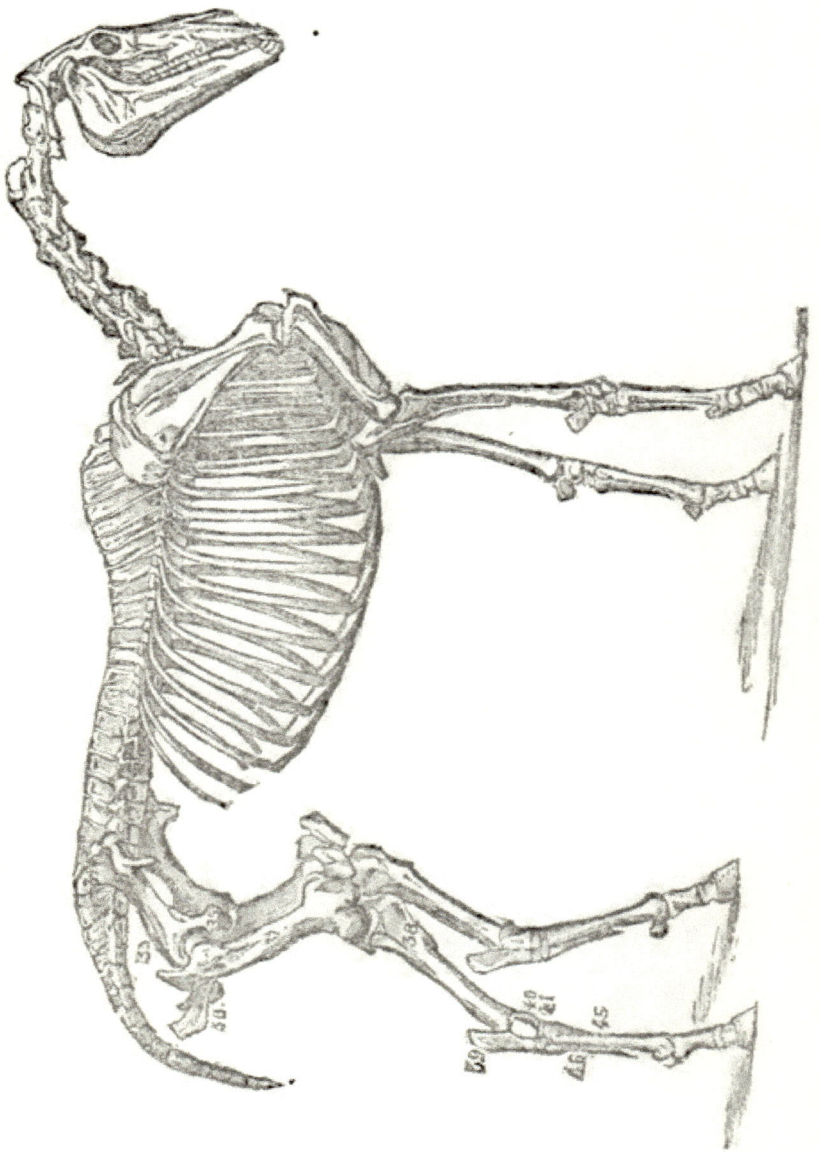

VERTEBRÆ.—The bones forming the neck and tail are seen to be without upper processes or spines. The remainder have spines. Those of the back proper having the *longest* spines, especially at the forward part known as the *withers*.

FORE EXTREMITY.—This is explained at Fig. 8.

HIND EXTREMITY.—33, 34, 35, 36 is the Ilio-ischium. 37. Femur. 38. Tibia, with the Fibula at the top of it and behind it. 39. Lever bone of hock, corresponding to the human heel, and called the *os calcis*. 40. The Gliding Bone, called *astragalus*, with its two large gliding surfaces well seen in the right hind leg. 41. Buffer bone of hock. 45. Metatarsal bone, with small metatarsals (46) immediately behind it. The remaining bones are the same as those of the fore leg.

LESSONS IN HORSE JUDGING.

LESSON I.

INTRODUCTION.

1.—In the following pages it will be attempted to place a subject which has hitherto been largely conducted empirically on a scientific basis.

2.—Horses are living machines like ourselves, and have many things in common with not-living machines, which obey certain well-known physical as well as physiological laws.

3.—Their mode of progression is by a system of levers, sometimes of perfect construction and advantageously disposed, but more often of imperfect construction and placed at a disadvantage.

4.—In order that the general student may follow us in our further remarks, it will be absolutely necessary for us to explain briefly the construction of these living levers, which are composed of two materials in every case, namely; an *active* material and several *passive* materials.

5.—The active materials are the so-called muscles of the body which we popularly call flesh or 'lean' meat. These muscles, which are attached to the levers of the body, and move them, in doing so always act in one and the same way—namely, by alternately lengthening and shortening. Of these two movements, one is *active*, the other *passive*. It is the *active* movement, that of *shortening*, which does the work. After a muscle has shortened, or, as it is termed, *contracted*, it allows other forces to pull it out or lengthen, it and it *passively* submits to being so lengthened.

6.—All muscles are made up of countless bundles, and these bundles are made up in fibres. These fibres being about the same size of all cases, it follows that the more of them the stronger will be the muscle, hence the larger the muscle the stronger. A muscle fibre (See Fig. 1. *C D*) is made up of a number of squares, placed one on the other, as you would place a pile of dice. These squares, on being stimulated, change their shape, as seen in the diagram. The power of changing their shape is called *muscular irritability*, and resides somehow or other in the muscle itself, or, in other words, every fibre has *irritability*. This *irritability* is called forth when a stimulant is applied. Various stimulants will call it forth. If you see an animal that is newly killed and which has its skin removed, you see the flesh twitch or quiver in various parts. This is the contraction or twitching here and there of the muscles, whose *irritability* is affected by the cold air, the cold air acting as a stimulant. If you now pinch one of the muscles, or prick it with a pin, it will quiver or contract. The same would occur if you applied galvanism to it.

The natural stimulants of the muscle are the *nerves* (Fig. 1. *n n*), the little white cords which you see running in various directions among the muscles or flesh, and which come from the brain and the spinal cord. If you had to apply a galvanic battery to a muscle, before long you would

Figure 1.

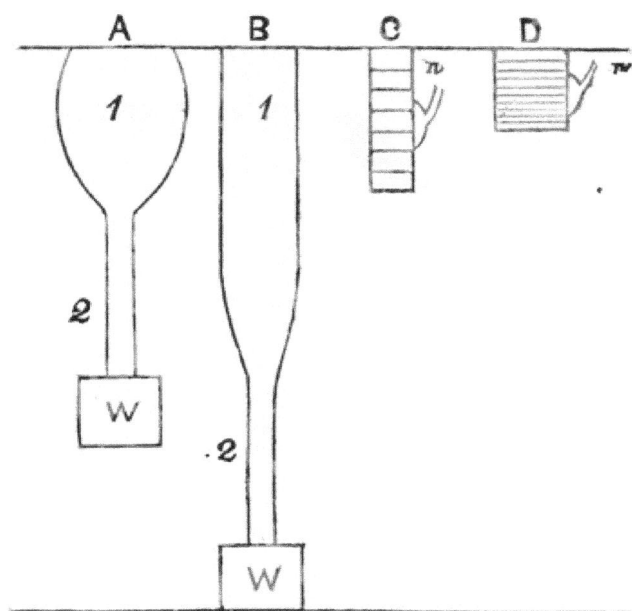

exhaust all its *irritability*, that is, in time it would cease to *contract*, showing that there is only a certain amount of *irritability* in the muscle. If all the muscles of the body contract at the same time, the whole body is perfectly rigid or stiff, a thing we never see in health, but which we see in a modified state after death, and which is called *rigor mortis.* This general stiffness, or *rigor mortis,* comes on as the body cools: the cold acting as a stimulant, as we have before seen. In a few hours or days the general stiffness disappears and leaves the body quite flaccid, that is, the cold has exhausted all the muscular *irritability*. In animals that are hunted to death, such as foxes, that are killed after being chased and able to run no further, or whose muscles have lost their *irritability* or power of further contracting, this *rigor mortis*, or stiffness of the body after death, never takes place. So it is with animals who die after long and exhausting illnesses, the stiffness after death either occurs, or occurs so slightly as hardly to be observed. Animals killed by lightning are also never stiff after death. The lightning being so powerful a stimulant as to exhaust the *irritability* of the muscles instantly.

7.—This irritability of muscle can be stored up in vast quantities when the muscle is in what is termed good *tone*. When we speak of a horse, a hunter for example, being *in condition*, we mean that his muscles are in good *tone*; or, in other words, that his muscles can lay in large quantities of *irritability*, which takes hours of hard toil to exhaust. The process by which the muscles are brought to 'tone' is called 'conditioning.' When large quantities of this *irritability* have been stored, the first expenditure of it is intensely pleasurable, and this pleasurable excitement, unrestrained, which it often is on first coming out of the stable, is called 'freshness.' Shortly, when some of the irritability or freshness has gone off, further expenditure of *irritability* causes neither pleasure nor pain, but indifference, and the horse is said to 'quieten down.' If the exercise or work be carried to an extreme, then, as the muscular *irritability* is vanishing, pain in the muscles comes on, which is nature's warning to stop the machine, and lay in another store of *irritability*.

S.—The part of the muscle which contracts is its red part, called its *belly* (Fig. 1. 1 1) and the hard, white glistening continuation of the *belly* is called the tendon (Fig. 1. 2 2). The *belly* of the muscle is usually attached to the fixed part, while the tendon is attached to the part to be moved. If, however, the part otherwise to be moved is fixed, and the muscle contracts, then the part to which the belly of the muscle is attached has to move. When the tendon is drawn towards the belly of the muscle and the movements again and again repeated, the parts would become heated by friction were it not that this is provided against. Friction is prevented by the tendon being surrounded by a *sheath*, containing a lubricating material called 'joint oil' or technically, 'synovia.' This 'joint oil' or 'synovia' is generated by a membrane lining the 'sheath,' and which gets the name of 'synovial membrane,' because it produces the synovia.

Some muscles do not terminate in rope-shaped tendons which have to 'play' through lubricated sheaths, but end in expanded sheet-like tendons which need no lubricating material. We shall find that the muscles of the face are of the latter description, and have their sheet-like tendons closely connected to the skin over the lips. This is well seen in ourselves in laughing. The *bellies* of the muscles forming our cheeks contract and of course swell out (Fig. 1. *A*), while their tendons are attached closely to the skin of the lips, especially the upper lip, so that in laughing the cheeks bulge out and the lips tighten and drag backwards.

9.—The contraction of a muscle is very limited, so that the tendon moves a very little distance in its sheath.

So much for the *active* part of the lever; the remaining parts are made up of *passive* agents in the form of bones and joints.

10.—Bones are of three varieties, named from their shape; long, flat, and irregular.

The long bones are largely concerned in forming the levers; as the fore and hind limbs, which are mainly composed of them. The flat bones, for the most part, make up the face and head; the shoulder blade is also a flat bone. The irregular bones make up the 'back bone,' called the 'vertebral column,' which extends from the head to the tip of the tail. The bones making up the 'back bone' are very numerous, being seven in number for the neck, eighteen for the back, fiv or six for the loins, five for the croup, and fron ten to twenty for the tail. With the exception of those forming the croup, which are stuck together and immoveable one on the other, the remainder of the bones forming this long column are slightly moveable one on the other, so that were you to pass a piece of stout cord down their central canal—which canal gives passage to the spinal cord—and hold one end of it high in the air, and shake it to and fro, it would wriggle like an eel. Other irregular bones are found making up the knee and hock joints.

11.—*Long* bones in forming joints have to expand at their ends (See Fig. 2. *A* 1), and these expanded ends are covered by a substance which

Figure 2.

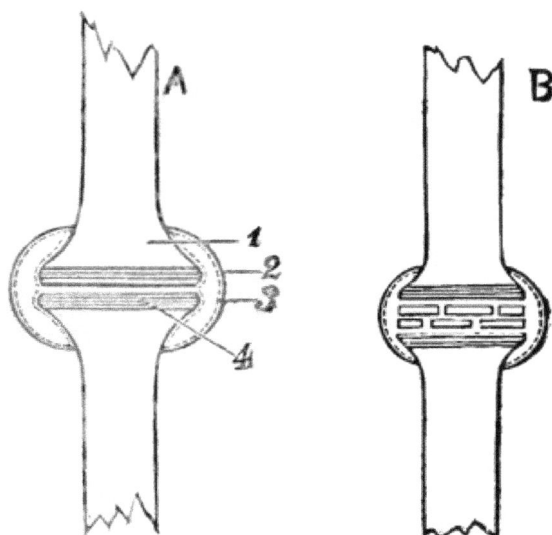

is yielding and elastic, and called 'cartilage' (Fig. 2. *A* 4) which acts like a buffer, and so lessens concussion. The two ends of the bone are bound to each other by strong unstretchable fibrous bands called 'ligaments' (Fig. 2. *A* 2). Oil is generated just as it is in the sheath of a tendon by a synovial membrane (Fig. 2. *A* 3), and is represented in our diagram by a dotted line. When a joint is subject to more than ordinary concussion; as, for instance, the 'knee' joint, provision

is made for additional cartilage by irregular **bones
being in**terposed between the two **ends** of the long
bones (Fig. 2. *B*), each of these bones being thickly
covered on its upper and lower surfaces, where
the concussion comes, by cartilage. So that in a
section from above downwards through the 'knee'
joint, instead of two buffers being interposed we
find six. The bone above the knee, and the bone
below it being in a straight line when the weight
of the body is thrown upon them, much concussion would take place were it not for this arrangement. When bones which meet and form a joint
are set at an angle, then of course there is less
chance of concussion, and so we find less 'cartilage' needed.

12.—As there are three forms of levers, we
must be careful to remember this, and we shall
close this somewhat dry and relatively uninter-
esting lesson by a few remarks on the *mechanical*
lever, and compare it with the *animal* lever.

The lever is an unyielding bar (represented in
the animal by bone), capable of free motion about
a fixed axis, called the 'fulcrum.' To this unyielding bar, 'power' is applied (which in the
animal **lever** is represented by muscle and its tendon). Lastly, we have the *weight, resistance*, or
obstacle to be overcome by the power.

If the fulcrum (*F*) be placed between the power
(*P*) and the weight (*W*), so that when the power
sets the lever in motion the weight and the power
describe *arcs*, the concavities of which are turned
towards one another, the lever is said to be of the
first order (See Fig. 3, *A*). If the fulcrum be at

one end, and the weight be between it and the power, so that weight and power describe *concentric arcs, the Weight moving through less space,* the lever is of the second order (Fig. 3, *B*). And if, the fulcrum being still at one end, the Power be between the Weight and Fulcrum so that the

Figure 3.

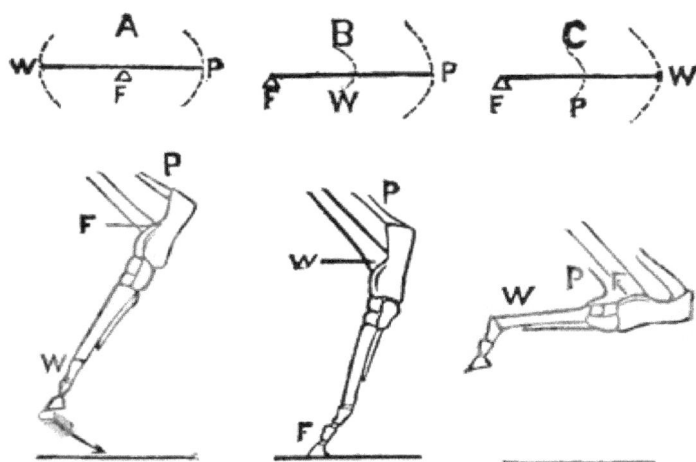

Power and Weight describe concentric arcs, *the Power moving through less space,* the lever is of the third order (Fig. 3, *C*).

We shall now give examples of these; first in mechanical levers:—

Lever of First order = the beam of the balance.

Lever of Second order = the common wheelbarrow.

Lever of Third order = the treadle of a lathe.

In the living lever we find one joint will illustrate all three orders according to its position with regard to the body. Let us take the hock-joint, in man called the ankle. We find, still referring to Fig. 3, that we have in the living lever a power in front and another behind the leg bone.

Now to illustrate our three orders of levers, we find we have only to study the hock-joint in the trot. The first order is seen in the hock in the trot *after* the foot has been lifted from the ground. To bring it quickly to the ground we find the *fulcrum* at the true hock-joint, the *power* attached behind to the point of the hock, and the *weight* to be moved, and all the parts below the hock, including, of course, the foot.

To illustrate our lever of the second order, take the hock in the trot *when* the foot is placed *on* the ground. We now find the fulcrum and weight have changed places, but the power is still as in the first order, *behind* the hock. The foot being planted on the ground is now the seat of the *fulcrum*, or fixed point, and the *weight* is the whole of the body which is thrown on to the true hock-joint, and is the obstacle to be overcome, and is being lifted and pushed forward.

Lastly, our lever of the third order is seen in the hock during the trot, when the hind leg is left behind after pushing the body forward, and has to be lifted and pulled forward before it can again be brought forward under the body (this is the same action, and better seen, when the hind foot is being lifted to knock of a fly that is irritating the belly), the front power is now acting, and the weight and fulcrum are the same as in the example of the third order, or, in other words, the power is in the middle.

Summarizing what has been said of the three orders of lever as exemplified by the hock-joint in trotting, we have found first, that the weight is all parts below the hock when the foot is *off* the ground, and all parts above the hock when the foot is *on* the ground.   Second, when the foot is off the ground and swinging backwards the lever is of the first order, but when swinging forwards it is of the third order, whilst it is of the second order when *on* the ground.

LESSON II.

THE NOSTRILS AND LIPS.

13.—The nostrils are those openings over the muzzle through which the air has to pass on its way to the lungs, and as a horse cannot breathe through his mouth, all the air he breathes *must* pass throught his nostrils, so that they must be as *wide* as possible.

The nostrils are made up of muscles, which are covered with skin and hair.

The muscles are for the purpose of regulating the width of the opening. It is plain that when the horse is at rest he needs less air than when walking, trotting, galloping, or drawing a load, and so only breathes about ten or twelves times a minute. In doing so, it is quite plain that the opening of the nostrils need not be so wide, as when at work he breathes three times as quickly. The muscles are thrown into action the moment the horse has to breathe more quickly, and you will have noticed the large, stiff and wide nostrils of a horse that is undergoing severe exertion.

14.—The opening of the nostrils when the horse is resting and breathing slowly is a mere chink or slit, but in violent exertion the nostril opening is quite round, and often reminds one of the mouth of that ancient weapon, the blunderbuss.

The muscles of the nostrils must be in good tone. All muscles, when unduly rested, lose their tone, but when only moderately used keep their tone. Perhaps of all the muscles of the body the muscles of the nostrils are the least likely to lose their tone, because the horse has only to walk quickly to be obliged to widen his nostrils and breathe quicker. Even in illness, the fever which so often accompanies his disease increases his rate of breathing, and so exercises the muscles of the nostrils. Sometimes, however, the muscles do lose some of their tone, and then, if you take and gallop the horse severely, the muscles vibrate and make a fr-r-r-r-apping noise. This peculiar noise disappears when the horse gets into regular work, and the muscle of the nostril acquires the requisite amount of 'tone.'

When the nostrils are a shade smaller than they ought to be and the horse is put to violent breathing effort, the muscles of the nostrils render the wall of the nostrils so stiff and rigid that the air in passing in makes a loud blowing noise, and clearly indicates want of nasal capacity. Such a one is called a 'high blower.' This is always a fault, and sometimes renders a horse worthless for violent effort, such as hunting, racing, and drawing extra heavy loads.

The nerve which supplies the muscles of the nostrils with the power of movement must not be overlooked. It comes from the brain and leaves the interior of the skull through a canal formed of bone, and close to the roots of the ears. You see it in the living horse on either side as it

passes over the cheek near the root of the ear as
three or four stripes as of thick whip-cord running
along under the skin towards the nostrils. This
nerve, after leaving the bony canal at the bottom
of the skull near the root of the ears, has to pass
through a gland, which produces the saliva or
spittle. It is this gland which swells at the side
of the face when he is said to have got the 'vives.'
In the horse, should this gland swell, it presses
upon the nerve we are speaking of, and stops its
current, and (as this nerve supplies the lips, the
muscle which closes the eye, also the principal
muscle of the cheek), when its current is quite
stopped these muscles become paralyzed and cannot move the parts, so that the lips hang down
and swing about like pendulums; the eye always
remains open with a fixed stare, and the cheek
bags out and the nostrils cannot become expanded.
All this can be brought about by a draught blowing on to the side of the head and giving a 'cold'
to the gland and causing it to swell and press on
the nerve. This state of things usually lasts from
one to three weeks, or until the 'cold' disappears.
The lesson we thus learn is this : see that the nostrils expand when the horse comes to exert himself, and also see that his lips are not swinging
about like pendulums. Very old horses sometimes have pendulous lips from debility. If you
are buying such a one give him a feed of hay,
and watch him to see if he can grasp the hay
with his lips, or if he has to push his nose into it
and seize it with his teeth. If he has to do this
don't buy him, because he will spoil more food

than he eats, from it dropping out of his mouth when chewing; he will take twice the time to feed, and he can never keep his condition. Sometimes he swings the lips about in trying to seize a morsel, showing that some power in them remains. If this be so, present a pail of water to him and watch him drink, and see if he can purse his lips naturally, or if they are so powerless that he has to dip his whole muzzle into the water nearly up to his eyes. If he cannot keep his lips pursed and so keep up a steady drinking effort, don't buy him.

15.—Next, hold his nostrils open and look inside. The pink, or it may be bluish red membrane you see, ought to be covered with spots of water like dew. There ought not to be any ulcers or abrasions to be seen, or 'raw' spots of any kind. You will always, however, find a very small opening like a 'punched out' hole, but this is natural, and no notice need be taken of it.

16.—If there be any discharge from the nostrils, save a slight watery discharge, it may be that the horse is suffering from a 'cold,' or he may be 'glandered.' The color of the discharge must be noticed, also its thickness. Then, again, you must notice whether it comes from both nostrils or only one. If it be from 'cold,' it may be variously colored, even green, as when the horse is feeding on green food in summer. It also may be of any thickness from wateriness to ropiness, and yet any be from a harmless 'cold.' If, however, it be thick and gluey, and sink when put into cold water, or be tinged with blood, it is most likely that the horse is glandered, and if so, he will inoculate you and so kill you, if you are not careful. The suspicion of glanders is strengthened if the discharge is coming only from one nostril.

If you are buying a horse, see that a discharge from the nostril is not cleaned away when your back is turned. The muzzle should have no streaks of discharge upon it, neither should it be wet as if sponged.

The bony nostrils is that part of the upper portion of the face between the muzzle and the eyes, and is immediately beneath the skin.

17.—The bony nostrils may be quite straight when the horse may be said to have a Grecian nose ; or they may be indented or pugged ; or they may be arched like a Roman nose. As *capacity* is so essential, it is evident that the Roman nose, though not the most sightly, is the best. A straight or Grecian nose is quite enough, if not too narrow. An indented or pug nose may also be capacious enough, but you must see that it is not narrow. If you suspect its capacity, you must remember the point when you come to examine the 'wind.'

THE MOUTH.

18.—As we have already said all that is necessary regarding the lips, we shall speak of the mouth as that cavity which contains the tongue and the teeth. The teeth are specially regarded in judging horses on account of their indicating the age. Horses, like ourselves, have two sets of teeth, one set for foalhood and a second for ma-

ture age.   The first are called 'milk' or 'temporary' teeth, and the second set are called 'permanent' teeth.   The teeth of the same mouth are
varied in position and shape, and receive different

Figure 4.

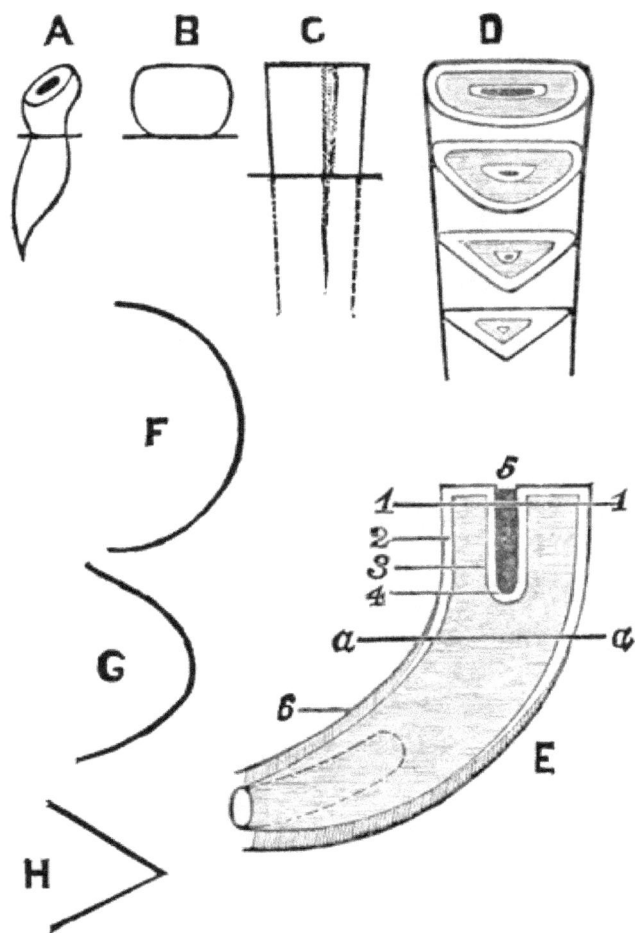

names.   The front teeth being called incisors or
'nippers;' the back teeth being called 'grinders;'
while between the two sets are the canine teeth,

which are called 'tusks.' As the nippers and tusks are most exposed to our view when we open the mouth, we pay most regard to them, so in speaking of the teeth we shall mean the 'nippers.'

17.—During the remainder of the lesson I must often draw your attention to the diagrams of Fig. 4 (page 27). So to begin: if you examine and compare a temporary tooth *A B* with a permanent tooth *C*, you will see well marked differences in *size*, *shape*, and *color*. If you look at the *front view* you will see that while the milk or temporary tooth is quite narrow near the gum (Fig 4, *B*) (which is represented by a straight line in the figure), the permanent tooth is seen to be nearly as wide at the gum as at the upper or cutting surface; so that a milk tooth is said to have a neck, whilst *a permanent tooth has no neck.* You will see the permanent teeth are a very little narrower at the part next the gum than they are at the cutting surface, or, in other words, they have *no neck.* Then again, the permanent teeth are very much larger than the temporary ones, and are not nearly so white. Then again, the temporary teeth are quite smooth on their front surface. Not so the permanent teeth. In the permanent tooth you see a groove, or perhaps two grooves, running from their cutting surface to the gum.

18.—Having determined which set of teeth you are examining, let us now consider the history of each set in its turn.

The temporary or milk teeth, are 'cut' in the following order: At birth, or a few days after, two *central* nippers appear. At six weeks old two other nippers appear, that is, one on each side of the two central ones. Between the sixth and ninth month two other nippers make their appearance, one on each side of the last ones ; and, as no others make their appearance, these are called the *corner* nippers, so that at last we have six nippers. Of course, six above and six below. Having thus cut the six teeth (and we are only speaking of one jaw), the foal is as a 'yearling' said to have a *full mouth*.

19.—During this first year, as might be expected, the nippers vary in appearance ; those cut first coming to maturity first, so that the central teeth which have attained their maturity at two months present a strong contrast to the ones next them at that time, which, as we have seen, are only a fortnight old. When the nippers are first cut, their upper cutting surface is sharp like a knife, and, this surface meeting the surface of the teeth in the other jaw, wears away until the broader part of the tooth is come upon, and then, instead of a sharp knife-like edge we get a flat surface like a table-top. Every nipper thus changes, alike in temporary and in permanent teeth. Therefore, at nine months old, or even at twelve months old, whilst the centre nippers and those next to them have more or less well marked flat table-top cutting *surfaces*, the corner nippers have still shelly knife-like upper *edges*.

The upper surfaces, worn flat, will be seen to have two distinct colors, but this we may quite disregard in the temporary teeth, and pay attention only to those appearances which we have already named.

It will be seen that during the first year the nippers are nearly useless because of the uneven surfaces of the teeth, some only being useable. Then again the mouth is very tender during the cutting of the teeth. During the second year the foal is in the full enjoyment of the services of his nipper teeth, which vary mostly in the *degree* in which they are worn down. Of course, the innermost ones being first cut, first come into use and are most worn down.

These temporary nippers begin to fall out or are shed at the age of two and a half years, or from that to three years, and are shed in the order in which they came; first, the central ones, and so on, so that we may say a foal has the use of his temporary or milk nippers from one year old to two and a half, or in other words, so far as his nippers are concerned, he has a 'full mouth' from one year old to two and a half.

20.—It is now time we began to study the anatomy of the permanent teeth in a rough and ready way. We cannot get out of it if we wish to be sure in telling a horse's age. Now-a-days teachers discard pictures as worthless, and teach by the aid of diagrams, so that you are not to feel your vanity touched by our using diagrams instead of pictures; for while you would find acres of diagrams in our great Medical and Veterinary Medical schools, you would be almost able to carry on your back all the pictures you would find. But the two are judiciously combined *sometimes*;

the diagram to show the broad outlines and more evident markings; the picture to exhibit the detail.

Still referring to our Fig. 4, if you examine a *permanent* nipper tooth, when it is extracted and you can see the whole of it, you see that it is bent almost in the form of a crescent, (Fig. 4, *E*). In describing the tooth, we must suppose it divided into two parts ; the visible part and the invisible part. The visible part is all that standing *above* the gums and is called the *crown :* the invisible part is that imbedded in the jaw and covered by the gums, and is called the *fang.* By studying the anatomy of a nipper tooth in a rough way, we can judge of a horse's age by the so-called 'marks' of his teeth. In Fig. 4, *E,* is a section down the middle of a nipper tooth from front to back. Let the line *a a* represent the line of the gums, then all above this is the 'crown' and all below it the 'fang.' The great bulk of the tooth is seen to be made up of the part indicated by the number 3, and is called the *dentine.* This substance has a coating of a substance termed 'enamel' (*E* 2), for the part of the tooth *above* the gum or the 'crown,' but where the tooth gets fixed into its bony socket in the jaw, the 'dentine' is not covered by 'enamel' as in the 'crown,' but by a very thin layer of bone, *E* 6, called 'crusta petrosa.' This is a long hard name, but we have done with it. Now pay attention exclusively to the crown of the tooth (the part above the gum line *a a*), and you see that the enamel *E* 2, after reaching the cutting surface of the tooth, dips into the tooth and forms a little sack-like cavity filled up with black material (*E* 5). Now suppose you cut off with a saw a piece of the cutting surface, say through the line *E* 1 1 then you see on the *surface* of such a section in their order either way :—

Enamel : Dentine : Enamel : | Enamel : Dentine : Enamel.

And you must remember the 'enamel' is white, and the 'dentine' gray. Now see if you can make out these in Fig. 4, *D*, which shows four sections of a tooth, such as we made at *E* 1 1. Notice the four sections of this tooth, and you see in the top section the appearances we have described very distinctly. You see the outer rim of white enamel which is called *encircling* enamel: then a broad circle of *gray* dentine: then a small circle of enamel called the *central* enamel, and this encloses the black material in the centre. So much for the top section, but before drawing your attention to the three sections below, I must first tell you that a nipper tooth gets *gradually narrower* from the cutting surface to the end of its fang, and whilst at its largest, from five or six years old to seven or eight, its upper cutting surface is somewhat ovoid, with the long axis from side to side having two sharp angles in front at either end. From this ovoid form it gradually becomes triangular, and it only remains to add that the depression in the tooth filled up by black material only reaches a little way down the tooth, and then you will be able to refer to the three lower sections of Fig. 4, *D*, to see the change in the aspects of the marks themselves and in the form of the tooth at each surface as the teeth wear down through age and use from a broad ovoid form to a narrow triangular form; and, as a consequence, in a very aged horse, the teeth do not present a compact mass when viewed from the front, but are more like so many pegs with spaces between them.

Lastly, on separating the lips of a horse in his prime, and viewing the closed teeth from the side, we see the large bold curve, as in Fig. 4, *F*; but as age advances and the teeth wear away, we get successively, but of course gradually, the curve *G*, then in extreme old age the angular curve *H*.

21.—We saw that with the milk teeth the central nippers came first, then the two next them— one on either side—and finally the two corner milk nippers, and at nine months old to a year at most the foal had a 'full mouth' of nippers. First come, first wear out; therefore the two central milk nippers are shed at two and a half years; the ones next these are shed at three and a half, the corner nippers at four and a half. So that at five years old—that is giving the corner teeth six months to grow up to having at least a cutting if not a grinding surface—the horse is said to have a full mouth.

Note.—The permanent teeth push out the temporary ones, in order to gain the situation for themselves. If the work of pushing out is done for them they come up easier and quicker. This gives rise to a process of 'forwarding the mouth,' as it is called, that is extracting the corner milk nippers of a three year old in order to hasten the arrival of the full mouth that a four year old may pass for a five year old. This is a gross cruelty, on account of the work of a five year old being expected of a horse only four. Should a permanent tooth not push straight at the fang of a milk tooth, the latter is pushed on one side, but not pushed out, and so remains by the side of the permanent tooth and may hinder the horse feeding to some extent. Such a tooth is then called a 'wolf' tooth. Wolf teeth are oftenest found in front of the front grinders.

LESSON III.

THE EYE.

22.—We now come to one of the four principal things which you have to see is sound and all right in buying a horse—namely, the eye. First take a glance at both eyes in good *daylight*, and compare their *size*. It is of the highest importance that they should be both one size, because if one is less than the other it is very likely that the lesser one has been attacked with inflammation which is called 'opthalmia.' Now 'opthalmia' is a disease that returns again and again, and destroys the sight. One of its effects is very often to leave the eye it has attacked *smaller* than its fellow. It also leaves other evidences, but these require a properly qualified veterinarian to discover.

The *color* of the two eyes may not be alike and yet the eyes may be quite sound. The color of the eye depends upon the coloring matter in the iris, a structure to be spoken of by and by. It may be absent in one iris, and brown or some other color in the other iris. The iris which contains no coloring matter will be white, and the horse is thus said to have a 'wall' eye. This white or 'wall' eye is as good as its fellow-eye, but it gives the horse an odd appearance which at best is unsightly, but still 'wall' eyes may be quite sound.

23.—Whilst you are looking at the eyes in broad *daylight*, notice if the *eyelids* are all right. Sometimes they get torn with projecting nails and are injured to such an extent that they cannot cover and protect the eye. Also notice if the tears run over the cheek. The tears are formed under the upper eyelid, but deep in the orbit or socket of the eye, and wet the surface of the eye and then find their way to the inner corner of the eye and thence through a canal into the nose. It occasionally happens that this canal gets blocked up, and then the tears cannot get into the nose and so escape.

When this is the case, they trickle out of the eye corner and over the face, and scald the hair off. This is often a curable condition, but very objectionable whilst it lasts. You will say 'how is it that we do not find the tears coming *out* of the nostrils if they escape into the nostrils as they do in the horse and in ourselves.' Well, because in health—except of course when we cry —the tears are only formed in sufficient quantity to keep the eye moist, just as the lining of the nose only forms sufficient watery material to keep it moist and no more. When there is more than suffices for the purpose we are said to have got a 'cold.'

24.—Having examined the eyes in broad daylight, you will have to examine them *with a candle* within a stable with the door shut. If you can have a choice, choose a stable that has a window above the stable door, as it will be a further aid in using the candle.

25.—Before going further we shall have to study the mechanism of the eye roughly, or we shall not understand what to look for and expect.

Figure 5.

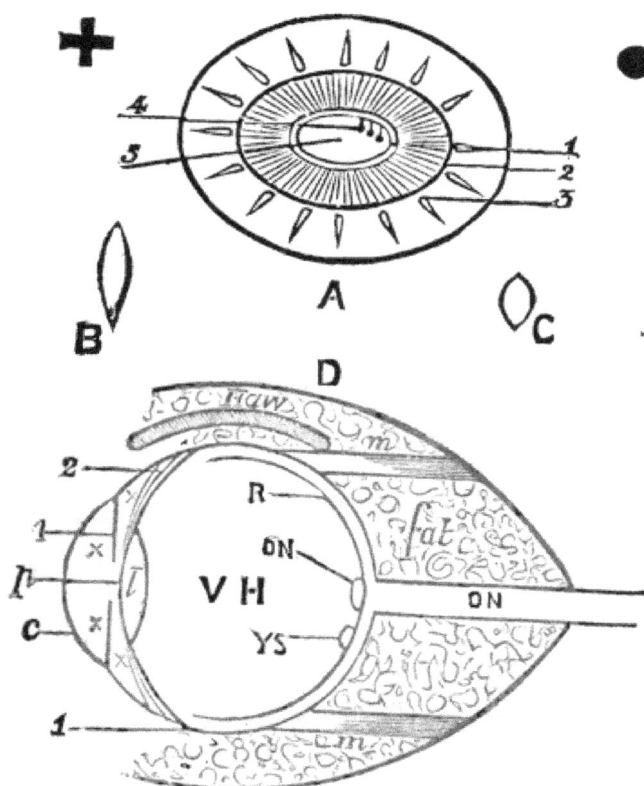

In Fig. 5 you find diagrams that will aid us in demonstrating the more important parts of the eye. When standing in front of the horse and viewing the eye, you can see an outer circle representing what is called the *white of the eye*, and is really the outer covering of the eyeball. Perhaps you will understand it better if we take an example. Suppose you take an orange, and cut a round piece of the skin or peel out about the size of a half-crown piece, the whole of the *peel*, or *skin*, which remains bears the same relation to the orange that the outer coat, or *white*, bears to the eyeball; that is to say, the skin which remains of the orange, and the white tunic of the eye in each case invests five parts out of six perhaps of its respective sphere.

We must make our orange do further service. When we have taken out the piece of the skin we find the white rind underneath. Take a penknife and cut a hole in this white part. the same as in Fig. 5 *A* 5; the hole we cut will represent the opening known as the 'pupil' through which the light passes into the eye. The remaining broad rim of white rind (Fig. 5. *A* 2) will represent the *iris*. Now if you have a watch-glass, the size of half-a-crown, and place it over the hole from which you at first cut the skin, the watch-glass will represent that glass-like covering of the eye which we call the 'cornea.' I fear we shall have to draw rather largely on our imagination to carry our illustration further. Let us see. Suppose you have a pair of spectacles with round glasses instead of oval ones, and you could remove one of these glasses, and (without rupturing our artificial 'iris') you could thrust it through the 'pupil' and place it immediately at the back of the 'iris,' this glass lens would then represent the 'lens' of the eye. Just a little further stretch of the imagination, then no more. When you took the lens out of the spectacles (in imagination of course) you found it surrounded by the iron, silver or gold *rim* which held it. You have placed the lens in the orange as described, and now in place of a metal rim around it, suppose we have a sheet-like muscle encircling the lens, and that the outer edge, all round, of this sheet-like muscle, is fixed to the interior of the orange peel a little further back than the lens.

We now look at Fig. 5, *D*, and we find the diagram of a real eye in section. Now, you will see the parts marked in the diagram as we have described them. First: the greater part of the outer coat (five-sixths we said) is formed by the *white tunic* of the eye called the *white* of the eye (Fig. 5, *D* 1). The remainder of the circle (our watch-glass) is the 'cornea' (Fig. 5, *D c*), then behind this we have the *iris D I*. Then behind this again the lens *D. l.* with its muscle, the *ciliary muscle* (*D* 2).

Let us describe the remainder of the eye by the aid of the lower diagram we are now looking at. That very large space marked *V H* is filled by a transparent jelly-like substance called the vitreous humor. Then you see the nerve of sight as it comes from the brain (*D, o n*) piercing the back of the white outer tunic like the end of a lead-pencil, and when it has gained the *inner* part of the tunic it spreads out like a sheet of tissue paper, and *lines* the back of the white tunic *inside* and is known as the 'retina' (*D R*). In this thin filmy sheet or 'retina,' close to the *optic nerve,* is a little body called the yellow spot (*D Y S*).

26.—So much for the eyeball. Now let us see how it is moved. The eyeball is imbedded in the bony skull in a socket or case, partly of bone, called the 'orbit,' and being very delicate, this bony orbit is filled with fat (Fig. 5, *D*), in which the eyeball is imbedded. In old horses and during illness this fat wastes away and allows the eyeball to sink in its socket. There are five or six muscles (Fig. 5, *m m*) to move the eye. The ends of each muscle are attached, one to the bony socket the other to the white outer tunic. We have only two of these muscles depicted on the diagram, but in real life one muscle is attached to the upper part of the eye ; one to the lower; one to the inner or nose side; one on the outer side. So that when the top one contracts the eye looks upwards, and so forth. There are two other muscles *obliquely* placed for rolling the eye, but these we will not consider. The four muscles named are called the four *straight* muscles, and when they all contract at once, the eyeball is pressed back into the socket and the 'haw' (Fig. 5, *D*), which is a thin piece of grissle also imbedded in the fat and whose edge can always be seen on the inner angle of the eye, is pressed or squeezed out of the fat and made to project over the eye.

27.—We must now turn our attention to the front half of the eye as we see it in the living animal, because it is this we have to examine with the candle in the darkened stable. Still referring to the diagram, let us study the parts in their order, beginning at the transparent 'cornea' (our watch-glass).

The light has first of all to pass through the cornea before it can pass through the hole we call the 'pupil,' and if the cornea receives any injury, as it often does from the whip, spots may be left which will split the light or otherwise daze the animal and make him shy. If, however, these spots are on the outer margin and not opposite the pupil, it is plain that the light will not be interfered with, or, in other words, the spots are of less consequence.

Covering the outer tunic or white of the eye, there is a very delicate membrane we have not mentioned, but which holds many blood vessels. This is called the 'conjunctiva,' and is that we see so red when the eyes are 'bloodshot.' If a hay-seed gets into the eye this membrane reddens, and the eyelids swell and are kept closed, and are suffused with tears. It is this membrane that is attacked in inflammation of the eye, so that you must see that it is not unduly red. In such horses there is a great quantity of dark coloring matter in it, so that the white of the eye is partly hidden behind it. This dark appearance is quite natural.

28.—We now come to the two most important structures of the eye, and without we know a good deal about them we cannot judge a horse thoroughly, but may be woefully cheated in purchasing a horse where we cannot call to our aid a skilled expert or veterinarian. The first of these two structures is the 'iris,' which acts like a curtain to a window, and is really the curtain of the eye. It is a very delicate moving muscle, flattened like a sheet of paper and ovoid, having an ovoid hole in its very centre (Fig. 5, *A* 5), which, as we have seen, is the 'pupil' of the eye through which the light passes. Now this hole, or pupil, varies much in size. When the eye is exposed to a bright light it becomes very small, but in the dark it enlarges to its widest. This is well seen in ourselves, but better seen in the cat. Put a cat before a window and you find the pupil diminishing almost to the size of a pin point. Then this muscle acts by enlarging or diminishing the 'pupil.' It does so in this way: Fig. 5, *A*, 2, represents the iris as viewed from behind. It is seen to be made up of inner circular fibres which radiate from these. When the pupil lessens, it is by the circular fibres contracting, but when it widens it is by the radiating fibres contracting. What we have to do in the darkened stable is to see that the 'pupil' diminishes and enlarges freely. For this purpose we cover the eye with our hand to darken it for half a minute or so when we expect the 'pupil' will dilate; then we place the candle close to the back of the hand that is covering the eye and suddenly remove the hand and watch the pupil contract, which it ought to do from the glare of the light being too much for the eye. In a darkened stable, and a candle held away from the eye, you will still see the pupil widening and narrowing, which is, of course, a sign that it is in good order and capable of acting as a curtain and keeping out bright glare, which dazes the animal. It widens and admits all light possible when there is not much light to spare. When the pupil is very widely open it gives the eye a glassy appearance, and should this condition be permanent, as you will have seen it, no doubt, the disease called *Amaurosis, gutta serena,* or *glass-eye* is present, and the eye is worthless. It may be from disease of the brain.

Instead of being fixedly open, the pupil may be fixed and quite immoveable and closed, or nearly so. This serious flaw arises in this way. When violent inflammation seizes the eye and attacks the 'iris,' a gluey discharge may occur from the surfaces of the 'iris,' and the back surface of the 'iris' may then become stuck to the fore part of the 'lens' (see Fig. 5, *I, l*).

If you refer to the diagram of the iris (Fig. 5, *A*), you will see two or three little black bodies hanging down (Fig. 5, *A* 4), swinging from the roof of the 'pupil.' These are quite natural, and appear in the eyes of many if not most horses.

We now come to the lens, which we represented by taking out a glass from a pair of spectacles. This lens (Fig. 5, *D, l*) is really placed close behind the 'iris' or curtain, and is for the purpose of *focusing* the rays of light so that they form images on the thin membrane we have before spoken of, called the 'retina.' Get a pair of spectacles, or a magnifying lens, and hold it in your right hand, and with it throw a bright light from a window, or a candle, or gas jet on to the

back of your other hand. Now move the lens
gently to and fro, and you will see a beautiful
little image of the window frame, gas jet, or
candle-light (whichever you are using) on the
back of your hand. Now you have got this perfect image by moving the lens backwards and
forwards between your hand and the light, and
you will have found that *correct distance* is
everything; that is to say, had you held the lens
an inch nearer or an inch further off, you would
not have got a sharp, clear image. Now look at
Fig. 5, *D*, and you will see that *behind* the 'lens'
there is the *V H*, or space filled with vitreous
humor, and in *front* of it there is the 'iris,' so
that it is quite evident that the 'lens' of the eye
cannot be moved backwards and forwards, an
inch forward now, an inch backward then, as
you have done in your experiment, because the
whole eye is only about an inch from front to
back, so that the focusing of the image on the
'retina' by the 'lens' must be accomplished in
another way altogether, and in this way the
shape of the 'lens' itself is altered.

29.—We must say a few words about the construction of the 'lens' of the eye, or you will not
understand what is meant by a *cataract*, so that
after we have seen how the 'lens' is made we can
see how it alters its shape in focusing. Turning
to the diagram Fig. 5, *D l*, you see that the *lens*
of the eye can be quite well represented by placing
two ordinary old-fashioned watch-glasses together
at their edges. Now, if you could fill the cavity
you thus form with stiff but very transparent

jelly, you would thus get a rough representation of the lens of the eye. Now, in the 'lens' of the eye, our two watch-glasses are represented by a very delicately thin pliable membrane called the 'capsule' of the lens, and so the whole 'lens' being firm, but pliable, can be altered in shape by the 'ciliary muscle,' (Fig. 5, *D* 2) which is, as we have seen, attached around its margin, so that when this muscle drags the lens backwards against the stiff 'vitreous humour,' the foremost half of the *capsule* of the *lens* (our foremost watch-glass) is bent like a bow that is having its string pulled in the act of shooting, and the lens is thus altered in its convexity from being shaped like *B* to being shaped like *C*, Fig. 5.

The lens of the eye is quite clear and transparent like glass, when in health; but from accident, disease, or old age, it may become opaque and *milky,* and then the eye is said to have a 'cataract.' 'Cataract' may occur from a horse falling on his head whilst hunting, or in rearing and falling back and knocking the head violently against the ground or by knocking the head violently against the top of a doorway—any violent blow on the head, in fact. It does so by rupturing the capsule of the lens (one of our watch-glasses) and letting in the 'watery humor' which occupies the front chamber of the eye, and which is marked *x x x x* in our diagram (Fig. 5, *D*). When the 'watery humor' gets into the substance of the 'lens' through a rent in the capsule, the 'lens' immediately begins to swell and become *milky* and *opaque,* and in a day or two the whole lens is swollen and white like milk. *Disease* causes 'cataract,' notably that disease in which a patient passes quantities of sugar with his water. *Old age* produces 'cataract,' by the lens shrinking and altering its proper structure.

When the 'cataract' is *complete*, that is to say, when the whole lens is affected, you see the milky white lens through the pupil, or in other words, the opening called the *pupil*, instead of being black as midnight, has a chalky or white appearance.

But the 'cataract' may not be complete; that is, only part of the 'lens' may be white and opaque. A 'cataract' may be no larger than a pin's head, and may be situated in any part of the 'lens.'

30.—To test the lens we use our lighted candle in our darkened stable. The test is called the 'catoptric test,' and is very easily applied. You take the candle and place it a little in front of the eye, a few inches from it, when you see *three images* of the candle-light; one upon the surface of the 'cornea,' one upon the front capsule of the 'lens,' (our front watch-glass,) and the third still further back, upon the hindmost capsule of the lens, (our hindmost watch-glass). Now, after you have distinctly found these three images, notice that the *two front* ones are *upright* like the candle-flame, but the *hindmost* image is *upside down*. After quite making out this fact, gently move your light from side to side, and you will see that while the two front upright images move in the same direction as the candle,

the hindmost one, which is turned upside down,
moves in the contrary way to the candle. It is
therefore evident that if the 'lens' is opaque and
milky you cannot see the hindmost or inverted
image, but you will only see the two foremost
upright images.

The cataract, as we have seen, may not involve
the whole lens, but may be just a little speck in
any part of it. Of course, if this speck be
towards the margin it may not split the light
and so be a detriment, but we never can tell how
long a small speck of cataract will remain small.
With practice you can detect these small specks
by the 'catoptric test,' but they are far more
easily detected with a little round mirror having
a little hole in its centre for you to look through,
which forms the reflecting part of every opthal-
moscope. Any one can use this very simple con-
trivance by holding it to his eye and reflecting
the rays of a candle into the eye—the candle
being held by the *side* of the head by some one
else.

We have seen that the 'iris' from inflammation may become stuck to the lens and so fixed.
But the 'iris' being a *moving muscle*, sometimes
drags and tears itself away, and in so liberating
itself, leaves bits of its structure upon the lens,
which will also appear like small cataracts. In
doing so it sometimes tears the capsule and lets
in the watery humor, and so causes cataract.

This ends our lesson on the eye. It only remains for me to advise close attention to what
has been said, and to advise the learner to take

every opportunity of verifying his knowledge and noticing the many infirmities he will meet with, and studying them by the broad light which we have here attempted to shed upon the subject. There are other methods of thoroughly examining the eye, but these are only of use to experts, surgeons, and veterinary surgeons, who are devoting their lives to such subjects.

Caution.—Do not mistake the optic nerve which can be seen through the *pupil* of the horse for a cataract, but which is distinguished by the 'catoptric test.'

Note.—The whole retina Fig. 5, *D* R, receives images except the end of the optic nerve itself. To prove this close your left eye by placing your left hand over it, then hold Fig. 5 at arm's length and look fixedly at the cross, and you see the black spot as well. Now, still looking at the cross, move it gently towards you, and as it approaches your face the black spot for a time ceases to be seen. The distance is generally seven or eight inches from the face.

LESSON IV.

31.—Having passed in review the nostrils, mouth, and eye, we must now review the face and head. We shall find that the face, as seen from the front, is of paramount importance in judging a horse, because the old saying, 'strength goes in at the mouth,' is as true to-day as it ever was. The saying, of course, has reference to the quantity and quality of food that is consumed. Now, no matter how much food is swallowed, unless it be of proper quality and so prepared by mastication or otherwise that the stomach can, in its turn, further advantageously dispose of it, strength will not follow. In order that large quantities of well masticated food may be swallowed, the back teeth, or 'grinders,' must have the following properties: they must have *large*, *flat*, and *regular* masticating surfaces.

But you will say, what has all this got to do with the front aspect of the face? The reply is, a great deal, but you are not asked to take this bare assertion on trust. It is of the highest importance that you should understand the conditions requisite for the 'grinders' to have *large*, *flat*, and *regular* masticating surfaces. But you will have to follow the description, as you did in the case of the eye, before you can understand.

The molar teeth or grinders (Fig. 6, A 1 1) are very large *cubical* blocks of bone which have to crush and grind down hard tough food, such as

Figure 6.

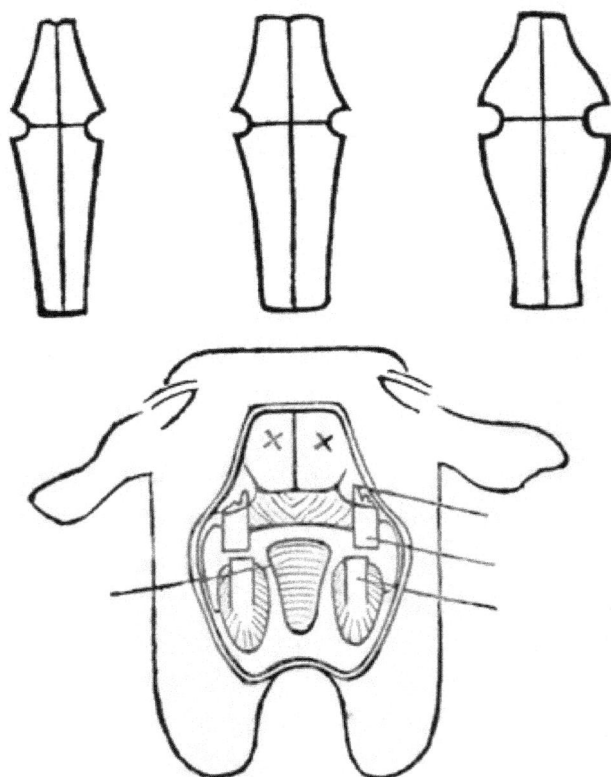

beans, oats and hay, and therefore require power-ful agents in the form of huge muscles to work them; so that, you see, where you have such large blocks and such large powers to move them, you must have *room* or *space* sufficient for both. But it so happens that *lightness* is also required, and greatest lightness implies least material, and with least material it must be disposed or shaped according to well-known geometrical laws; if you require the three conditions in one, namely, *size*, *strength*, and *lightness*, these geometrical laws are carried out *at the expense* of *room* or *space* if not in one direction, in another.

If you refer to Fig. 6, *A*, you will see a perfect model of lightness and strength. It is the diagramatic representation of a section of a horse's head and jaws carried from above downwards across the head, somewhat below the eyes. The four pieces marked *I I I I*, represent four molar teeth or grinders, two in the upper and two in the lower jaw. They have all flat table-top grinding surfaces, the top one meeting a corresponding bottom one. Those of the lower jaw are set in solid bone, which is rendered light by being shaped like the letter *V*, that is to say, having two branches meeting below. The front part in our diagram being removed, we can only see the section of the two parts of the lower jaw each holding a molar. Above the upper jaw are the large passages through which the air passes *A x x*, and are nearly hollow and form the back part of the bony nostrils, but the cavities *Y Y* are only there to allow of the bone being as light as possible, and as cavities are quite worthless. The upper jaw forms an arch, having substantial buttresses in the molar teeth and their bony sockets, and whose span is of gigantic strength and extremely light from its hollow construction.

If you notice a horse eating, you will see that the lower jaw is pressed upwards against the upper jaw, and moves from side to side. If the movement of the lower jaw on the upper one were a simple up and down movement, then the muscles could be *perpendicularly* placed and their bulk only allowed for, but seeing that the lower jaw has to be moved from side to side, the muscles have to be *obliquely* placed and so necessitates the branches of the jaw being wide apart at their hindmost part. But the lower grinders are somewhat narrower than the upper and so allow greater range of motion in grinding, so that *breadth of the upper jaw is essential* as well for allowing free masticating power, as for power to breathe freely through wide enough openings.

32.—This then *necessitates* width between the eyes, and width between the lower jaws. In the figure illustrating this lesson you will find three diagrams, *B, C, D*, representing front face views of three degrees of width. What has been said will explain why narrow-faced horses are often weakly, with narrow chests and long legs, and disposed to have 'thrushes' in the 'frogs' of their fore feet, and are also prone to diarrhœa. It would be beyond the province of this little book to enter into a lengthened explanation of these coincidences and shorter explanations would not suffice.

33.—The side face should be deep for the same reasons that the front face between the eyes should be broad, that is, for roomy nostrils above and for the efficient setting of the massive grinders.

34.—*Length* of head is not of such importance. It cannot well be too short so far as the chief requisites are concerned. When we find very narrow faces, we frequently find length of face great.

35.—The so-called forehead of a horse is the space bounded below by a straight line drawn between the eyes, above by roots of the hair of the forelock, and at the sides by the large muscles which lift the lower against the upper one. The breadth of the forehead depends upon the breadth between the eyes and the size of these muscles. It is almost impossible to judge the size of the brain in the living horse by breadth of forehead. Size of brain is no index of character in either horse or man. In either case, we can only judge of a brain by the quality and quantity of the thought, and so forth, it produces, so that we need not dwell further on the physical aspects of the head.

36.—The eyes should be as *large* as possible, and not be obliquely set in the face as in the Chinese. In long, narrow-faced horses we sometimes find this obliquity of the eyes, and this is an additional flaw.

37.—The white of the eye should not be too conspicuous. When too conspicuous it gives to both man and horse a *wild stare*, and is an almost unfailing sign of mental aberrations, which lead to acts which we characterise as vice, such as biting, kicking, &c. The white of the eye is

seen, not on account of there being more of it
than usual, but on account of the eyelids being
wider apart.   This condition is known to doctors
as the *insane eye*, and is seen by the least observ-
ant by attending Divine worship in any lunatic
asylum chapel and sitting near the parson.   This
condition has been so connected with viciousness
in the horse, that in Yorkshire it is a common
expression among horsemen, "He shows too
much of the white of his eye for my money."   I
would, however, guard you against condemning
all horses with this form of eye as vicious, but
have a special warranty against vice in purchasing one, and at all times avoid such when you
conveniently can.

38.—The space between the lower jaws near
the top of the neck cannot be too wide, for
reasons we have before seen.   There is also
another reason why the branches of the lower
jaw should be wide apart.   The top of the windpipe ends in the *speaking box* called the 'larynx.'
It is much larger than the remainder of the
windpipe, and in men can be seen and felt as a
large hard prominence which moves up and
down when we swallow.   It is also called
pomum Adami, or Adam's apple.   When the
nose is held in towards the neck by the bearing-
rein being over tight, this delicate box, which is
made up of pieces of hard cartilage, moved by
numerous delicate muscles, gets pressed out of
shape and causes roaring, or grunting, or trum-
peting.

This box is quite between the branches of the

jaw in most positions of the head, and is a most delicately organiezd structure, and therefore soon thrown out of order, causing the above noises in moving. Now there is a disease called the Strangles affecting young horses, in which a gathering or abscess takes place in the space between the jaws, and therefore close to this delicate box, the 'larynx.' During the time the abscess is ripening there is necessarily great inflammation about this box, and if it lasts unduly long by being treated by so-called 'home' remedies, or worse still by the farrier, the inflammation is apt to injure the delicate little muscles of which the box is partly composed, and leave the animal a 'roarer.'

39.—All badly treated gatherings or abscesses are apt to leave behind them two evidences of their former presence, viz: thickening of the skin and parts beneath, and ragged scars. Therefore, always look for these between the jaws of a horse. The skin in this situation should be fine, the hair silky, and you ought to be able to bury your stretched out hand, laid lengthwise back uppermost, in this space: or, in other words, see that the space between the jaws be not *flush* with the lower borders of the jaw.

40.—The ears, forming part of the head, may here be noticed. They ought not to be too large, indeed they can hardly be too small. They vary in shape slightly, but very little.

LESSON V.

The neck of the horse may be roughly stated to be an oblong, having the bones of the neck or cervical vertebræ as a diagonal; thus, (Fig. 7, *A*). We have thus a rough idea of its fundamental structure, and shall be able further to discuss the subject intelligibly. The column of bones is represented by the diagonal that divides the neck above and below into two triangles, the upper one being the larger and more clearly defined. On referring to Diagram *B* it will be seen that this upper triangle contains the great cervical ligament which supports the great overhanging mass formed by the head and neck. It will no doubt often have occurred to non-anatomists, as a matter of wonder, how such a weighty overhanging mass as that of the head and neck gets supported, and how it is kept from dropping down and dangling between the fore legs. It will be seen on reference to Fig. 7 *B* that there is a ligament occupying the upper triangle of the neck which has *two distinct forms*, a cordiform or funicular portion, 1 1 1, and a lamellary portion, 2 2 2 2. The former is continuous, with the ligament running along the upper ends of the spines of the vertebral column of the back and loins, and then stretches along the upper part of the triangular space of the neck and gets inserted to

Figure 7.

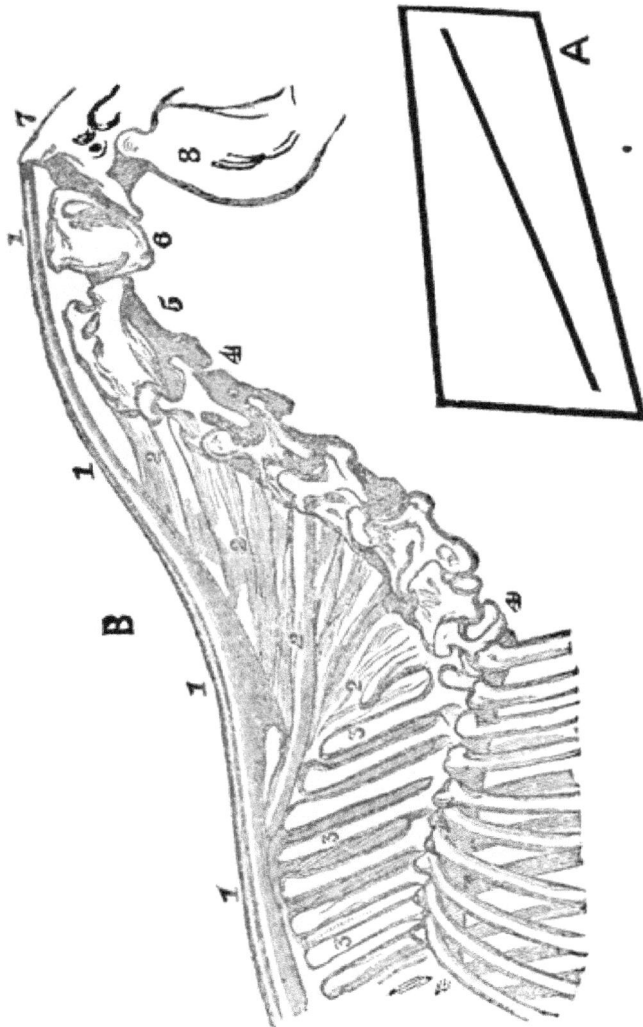

the summit of the head at the back; whilst the other portion spreads from above downwards like

a fan and in reality is given off from the upper
or cordiform portion. This fanlike portion has
six slips, which get inserted to the spines of the
last six of the bones of the neck.

In the first lesson we saw that muscle was an
active contractile tissue *which could become exhausted*, so that if the neck and head were supported by muscles, after a certain time, the head
and neck would drop. This is never the case, because they are supported by the ligament we
have been describing, which is made up of a con-
gregation of elastic fibres which are devoid of
feeling, and therefore are never tired and are
quite as passive as so much india rubber, that is,
the ligament stretches when anything stretches
it and recoils when the stretching force is removed.

The next thing I must direct your attention to
is that the cordiform or upper part of the ligament is *broad* at the top, and that the skin of the
neck is separated from it by a quantity of fat imbedded in fibrous partitions. The amount of fat
placed upon this ligament varies greatly. In the
clean, light neck of the hunting gelding this fat
is barely represented, whilst in low-bred animals,
in stallions, and in those which have been cas-
trated, after two years of age or after the procre-
ative organs have assumed their functional activity, this fat and fibrous tissue lying along the
cordiform tendon on the upper surface of the
neck is of considerable thickness and forms a
'crest.' It is of course best seen in stallions, and
gives their neck its peculiar shape. In the

heavy, soft cart horses which are largely im-
ported into Great Britain from Belgium it is also
a prominent feature. Some colts are purposely
left till two years old before castration, on purpose to develop this fat and 'give them a neck,'
as it is called. The quantity of this fibro-fatty
substance in the neck principally, but not entirely, makes the difference between a gross
'fleshy' neck, and a fine clean neck, and when
it is stated that there is no strength in this fibro-
fatty mass, it need hardly be added that a clean,
light muscular neck is as powerful as a gross,
thick, heavy neck, which is largely made so by
this stored up fat; only, of course, the possessor
of the latter can throw more weight into a collar,
and is so far preferable for draught purposes.
Besides judging of the quantity of this fibro-fatty
structure by the sight, you can grasp the top of
the neck, feel its thickness, and shake it from
side to side.

41.—On each side of this ligament there are
powerful muscles which fill up this upper triangular space and get attached to the bones of the
neck, especially to the last five of these. We
have seen that the bones of the spinal column
have little movement *individually*, but *collect-
ively* the column has considerable movement,
which we likened to the wriggling of an eel.
There are very small muscles which stretch from
every bone of the column to the next bone in
front of it, and are said to 'clothe' the spinal
column. These muscles of themselves cause the
wriggling movement of the column. The col-

umn, however, is acted upon by other muscles than those little ones stretched from bone to bone. These muscles are among the largest and most powerful muscles of the body, and bend the bones of the neck very much upwards, as in taking hay out of racks placed very high, or very much downwards, as in grazing. The part of the vertebral column forming the loins is also much bent in galloping and leaping, but the most movement is in the column forming the tail.

Shortly reviewing what we have said regarding the movements of the back-bone or vertebral column we have found that it can *move itself*, and that it can *be moved*. That in moving itself it does so by the little muscles which clothe it, and that the amount of this movement only amounts to what we have, somewhat inelegantly, termed a wriggle. That *in being moved* by muscles from without, the motion is far more extensive. Lastly, we found that there was most movement in the tail, the next in the neck, and then in the loins, so that we have only to add that there is next to no movement in the back, and as has been mentioned, the bones of the croup are glued together and quite immovable.

Having said enough for the present about the 'back-bone' or 'vertebral column' in general, I wish now to fix your attention upon that portion of it, made up of seven bones, forming the neck. In the fore part of this lesson we saw that the bones of the neck ran diagonally, from below up-

wards and forwards, and we have since seen that
whether it is straight or curved depends upon the
action or inaction of certain muscles. When the
horse is standing quietly at rest the elastic ligament simply suspends the head and neck, and in
doing so the bones of the neck are nearly
straight, having only the faintest possible curve,
or in other words, the neck at rest is at its
straightest. When the neck is not at rest, the
bones of the neck will be bent according to the
attitude of the horse, and, as we have seen, the
muscles filling the upper triangle, being inserted
into the hindmost bones of the neck, are most
concerned in altering its shape.

Referring to Fig. 7, *B*, we find that the hindmost side of the upper triangle depicted in Fig. 7,
A, depends for its depth upon the length of the
'spines' of the bones of the vertebral column of
the foremost part of the back. This part, horsemen know as the 'withers.' It therefore follows
that the higher the withers the greater the power
of raising and bending upwards and backwards
the bones of the neck, or in other words, *the
higher the withers the greater the power of holding up the head and neck.* So that with high
withers, that is, with a *deep* triangle, the large
muscles of this region not only act with the least
expenditure of power, but the efficiency of space
from above downwards enables large muscles to
occupy this region without making the neck
thick, because great and powerful muscles can
be stowed away in a space which though narrow
is very deep; whereas for the same bulk, and as

we have seen strength, to be stowed away in a less triangle, the space *laterally* has to be encroached upon. So that given the same weight of head, and strength and length of neck, the higher the withers the thinner from side to side will be the neck, hence we find as a general thing that horses with low withers have more, so-called, fleshy necks than those with high withers, because these muscles are stowed and have to act at a greater disadvantage.

THE NECK AND HEAD.

42.—We have next to consider the neck and head together as weights and as fulcrums, also as power. The head as a whole may be regarded as a *solid mass* attached to the foremost part of the neck at a *variable* angle. The upper and foremost part of the bones of the neck meets the head at its very top, (Fig. 7, *B*) that barely two inches of the head is above the bony juncture of the head and neck.

By this arrangement we get a lever of the first order which moves the head as a rigid bar up and down, the neck being fixed and acting as a fulcrum. The upper arm of the lever, we have said, is about two inches in length only, and so allows it, whilst moving through very little space itself, to move through great space the lower and longer arm of the lever made up at the head generally. The head has a side to side movement also, but we shall not stop to consider it in any way because we think our ends may be gained without this. Again reminding you of what was said about the superior triangle of the neck being occupied by muscles, which get attached to the last five bones of the neck, and of course when acting draw these bones upwards and backwards, there are positions, as for example, when the horse during the act of leaping a height is in a rearing attitude, and poising the body the instant before taking the spring, when the neck has to be drawn upwards and backwards, and the muzzle drawn well in to the neck, in order that the face may be conveniently situated for the animal to look straight down upon the object to be leaped over. In such a case the neck assumes the most marked double curve. The hindmost curve is first produced in the way we have mentioned, and the bones of it being fixed allows the part to become a *fulcrum* for the muscles acting at the lower side of the neck to draw the muzzle backwards. We have next the neck in one long curve, and the head extended as when the horse is feeding out of a very high hay rack. Next we have the neck straight and the head extended, as in the race-horse during the hottest part of the race nearing the winning post, and, as we have seen, the neck and head may be at rest and almost at right angles.

In our first lesson we saw that muscles, when in the full enjoyment of their highest functions, were said to be in *tone*. We have also seen in this lesson that muscles alter the curve of the vertebral column, more especially those parts of it forming the neck and the tail, so that it follows as a corollary that if the muscles of the neck habitually act in one position more than in any other position, the neck will become more and more moulded into that position. Hence we see the seasoned carriage-horse with powerful highly developed muscles of the neck, which gives to his neck a more massive appearance with its double curve. The bearing rein, judiciously applied, effects this by compelling the horse to keep his head up and his nose in, which no doubt is tiring at first, till the muscles of the neck get into condition; just as in the case of the raw recruit who has to keep his head up, shoulders well back, and the palm of the hand open to the front. The muscles in six weeks or less get into tone, and there is an end to pain from restraint.

The bearing rein does this good, it causes development of the muscles of the neck, and enables greater weight and strength to be thrown into the collar. Consequently it enables those who drive pairs to have both breeding and substance.

In concluding this lesson, we have just to remind the reader that the neck has two sources of bulk, namely, the fibro-fatty mass which we have before discussed, and the forced development of the muscles. So that we may have both these conditions in the same neck, or one only.

We shall have more to say about the head and neck in our next lesson.

LESSON VI.

The general student may not know what is meant by the fore extremity, so I shall have to explain it. Our arms and hands are called our upper extremities, our legs and feet our lower extremities. The words upper and lower being used on account of our upright position of body. Quadrupeds having horizontally placed bodies are said to have fore and hind extremities, corresponding to our upper and lower ones.

43.—The horse's fore extremities are made up of all three kinds of bones, long, flat, and irregular. The topmost bone is a flat bone, and the only flat bone, and is called the 'scapula' or 'shoulder-blade.' All the other bones are of the long kind, except the little bones in the so-called 'knee' joint, we have before alluded to in paragraph 11, and one or two little bones we shall afterwards speak of.

The bones of the fore extremities are of *various lengths,* and from the top of the arm bone down to the foot they *gradually lessen in thickness.* Also please to notice that the so-called 'knee' joint is a misnomer, as it is the part corresponding to our wrist joint, and has the same number

Figure 8.

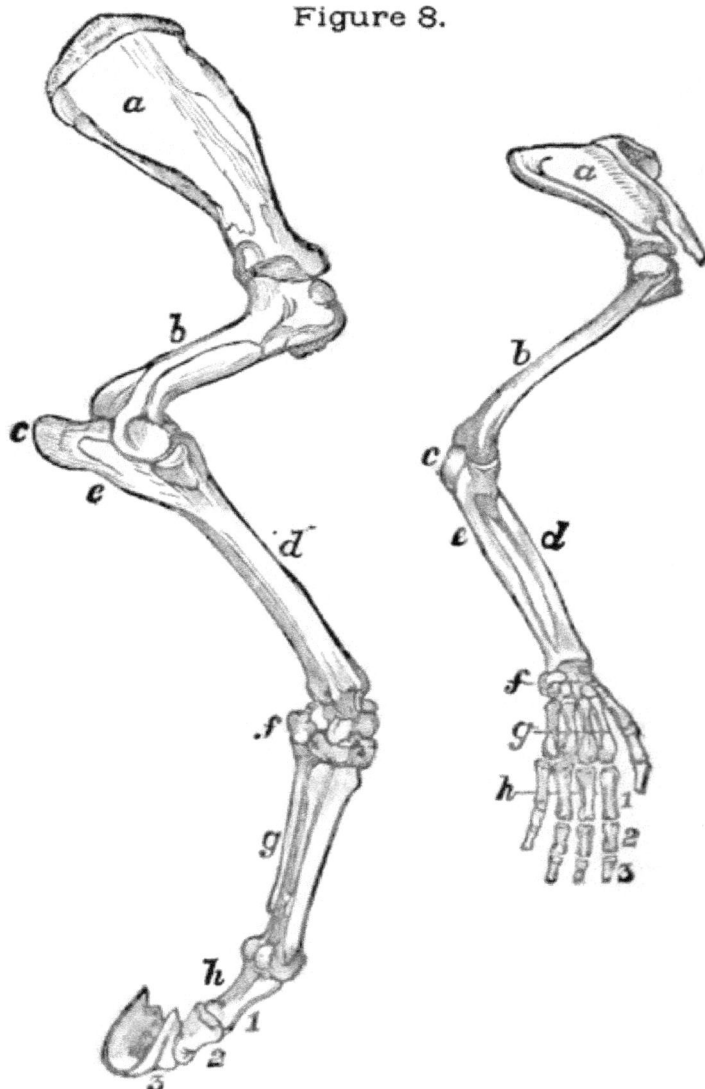

Fore extremity of horse.

a. Scapula, or shoulder blade.
b. Humerus, or arm bone.
c. Elbow.
e. Ulna.
d. Radius, or bone of forearm.
f. Carpus, or knee (wrist.)

Upper extremity of man.

g. Metacarpal bones.
1 2 3. Phalanges.
h 1. First phalanx or suffraginis.
2 Second " or coronal.
3 Third " or pedal.

of bones in it and of the same shape nearly, but larger. From our wrist joint five lengths of bone proceed, but in the horse, who is a *solipede*, only one length proceeds. This one length faithfully represents our middle finger from the wrist joint to the tip covered by the nail. Now, beginning at the shoulder-blade and going downwards, let us compare our extremity with its homologue, as anatomists call it, in the horse. You are not to be impatient and question the use of it, until you have patiently waded through what I have got to tell you, and then say whether it is of use. The two extremities are given in Fig. 8.

44.—The scapulæ of man and horse are both flat bones and both triangular bones, with a very strong ridge of bone running down their middle or nearly down their middle. This ridge of bone serves many purposes. First it strengthens the bone without adding materially to its bulk, just as the engineer shapes his iron which has to bridge across a space and to bear great weight, and have as little weight as possible. Second, you notice this 'spine,' as it is called, is less in proportion in the horse than it is in man, and that in the horse it is not continued into a long, strong process. The reason of this difference is that the horse only uses his fore extremities to walk with; he has no 'collar' bone or 'clavicle,' as it is called by anatomists. Now the collar bone is a long bone at the top of our chests in front, shaped like the old-fashioned letter *s*, like this *ſ*, and it has one end placed against the top and side of the breast bone, but its other end

meets the extreme tip of this spine of the scapula
and props the shoulders back, and so keeps our
shoulders well back at all times. Were it not for
this bone, when, in using our arms, we stretched
them forward, there would be nothing to prevent
our two shoulders almost meeting in front. It is
the relative length of this bone that determines
the appearance of our shoulders. If growing
children are allowed to sit with their shoulders
huddled up, the two ends of this bone are unduly
pressed upon, and the double curve is increased
and the collar bone more bent, and, as a consequence, more shortened, and the shoulder blades,
not being duly propped back, stick out behind,
and the child grows up 'round shouldered.' It is
owing to the slightly greater length of this bone
which gives Frenchwomen their more graceful
shoulders and chest. Lions, tigers, cats, &c.,
use their fore extremities for seizing things and
holding them, so that they have clavicles or collar
bones like men and women. A third use of this
'spine' of the scapula is that it acts as a fulcrum
or fixed point for muscles, also as a place for insertion for tendons.

45.—The next bone, called the 'humerus' or
arm bone, will be seen to be exactly alike in both
cases, only it is relatively very much longer in
man. In both it is a powerful bone, but especially so in the horse. Extremely large muscles
clothe it.

46.—The next two bones are the radius and
ulna. In man, both these bones are continued
from the elbow joint to the wrist as *separate*

bones, but you will notice that in the horse the ulna, after helping the radius to form the elbow joint, coalesces with the radius, so that the two in a full grown horse look like one bone. This being so, the ulna is said to be *rudimentary* in the horse.

47.—The bones of the carpus are nearly alike in both, only, of course, larger in the horse. We shall call this the knee as usual, although, as you see, it is the wrist.

48.—There are five metacarpal bones in our hands, but the horse has only one which is fairly represented by the metacarpal bone belonging to our middle finger. You see two small metacarpal bones in the horse, but these are dwarfed and only *rudimentary*, and in the very aged, stuck to the larger 'metacarpal.' Notice, though, that the tops of all three articulate with the bones above them, *i. e.*, with the lower bones of the 'carpus' or 'knee.'

49.—The remaining bones explain themselves almost. Taking the bone in our middle finger from the knuckle to the first joint, we find it corresponding in everything but size to the long pastern bone of the horse.

50.—The next bone to this again corresponds with our next bone in the middle finger, but is relatively very much shorter and broader.

51.—The last bone is very highly developed in the horse, and is called the pedal or 'coffin' bone. In ourselves it is little more than rudimentary, on account of its not being called upon as a lowest point to bear the weight of our body. We can very distinctly see the resemblance it has to the same bone in the horse in the skeletons of those who, during life, used their fingers in hard, heavy toil.

52.—The next three bones are sessamoid bones, and are very specially more related with the long tendons which stretch from the back of the knee to the foot.

So much for the 'bars' of our levers which we saw were in the animal, the *bones*. Now for the *powers* of the animal levers which we saw were the muscles with their tendons.

53.—On referring to Fig. 8, *E*, it will be seen that we have the bones of the fore extremity hidden or clothed by their muscles. This, however, is a picture or a faithful representation of the parts as they are in reality, and as the origins (fixed points) of the muscles and their insertions (moveable points) are very numerous, it will be useless to describe the origin and insertion of each muscle, but by the aid of diagrams we can see these living levers to greater advantage. I will, however, draw your special attention to two things. First, you ought to get a mental picture of this Fig. 8, *E*, in order that you may be able to recognize it as seen in the living horse, covered, however, by the skin. Secondly, please to notice that all the parts from just above the the 'knee' are made up of the *bellies* or contracting parts of the muscles with hardly any visible tendon, but that from just above the knee to the foot all is tendon and bone together, not a single *belly* of muscle. Perhaps there is a third point you had better notice, namely, that of the bulky fleshy part, the greatest bulk is at the back of the shoulder blade and arm bone, the shoulder getting more and more bulky as it descends. Look steadily first at the column of bones unclothed until you can see them in your mind's eye through their fleshy clothing, because I give you warning that we are now going to represent all we have got to say further by straight, bare lines only.

54.—Before going any further, we must revert to the dry subject of levers. Let me impress upon you this universal law, that power and speed are always related to each other, but that this relation is always *antagonistic*. Expressed in other words it is this, 'if you gain power you lose speed,' which is only saying, of course, that 'if you gain speed you lose power.' This universal law does a great deal for us by acting as a wholesome check to our enterprise. Were it not for this antagonism we should build ships that would convey cities instead of their present modest loads, and these would run at speed calculated by seconds instead of days and weeks and so forth. This law has existed, and will exist, through all time. We, however, try to unite the two things as closely as possible ; the 'Great Eastern' steamship for example. This *artificial* combination is nowhere more striven after than in our breed of horses, the English hunter for example.

55.—We shall make this antagonism between *power* and *speed* do us good service here. It enables us to include every horse under the sun under three logical divisions, namely:

1.—Horses of Speed, *e.g.*   Racehorses.

2.—Horses of Power, *e.g.*   Draughthorses.

3.—Horses of Power and Speed, *e.g.*   Hunters.

It is apparent that the first two, being extremes, will be in the minority, because most of our wants require a combination of power and speed.

56.—We must just allude to one other point, and that is the rhythm of movement. Let us take a simple movement, such as walking, and see what the fore extremities do and are down to in this rhythm. It will be seen on reference to Fig. 9, A, that an attempt has been made to represent this rhythm by a diagram which really represents two rhythms. It will be seen that either rhythm is included in a parallelogram made up of two *equal* triangles, a' a'' a''' and a'' b'' b'''. They are equal because they are on the same base, a''' b''', and between the same parallels a' b'', a''' b'''.

It will be seen that a rhythm is begun when the foot is on the ground, as at b''', and completed when the foot reaches the ground, as at a''', and the limb has gained the same relation to the body (represented by the arrow), as at a' a'''. Take the parallelogram a' a'' b''' a''', then it will be seen that the leg is flexed and extended within the triangle a''' a'' b''', and that the body swings forward and brings the leg from position a'' a''' to a' a''', and this movement is accomplished within the triangle a' a'' a'''. It is needless to remind the reader that in the walk one fore foot is on the ground when the other is off it, therefore the fellow leg is bearing the body's weight whilst the foot is being put from b''' to a'''.

In passing forward the foot from b''' to a''' the leg is

1.—Flexed.

2.—Dragged forward whilst flexed.

3.—Then extended.

Now we saw that the spinal column had its own intrinsic muscles by which it moved itself, and

Figure 9.

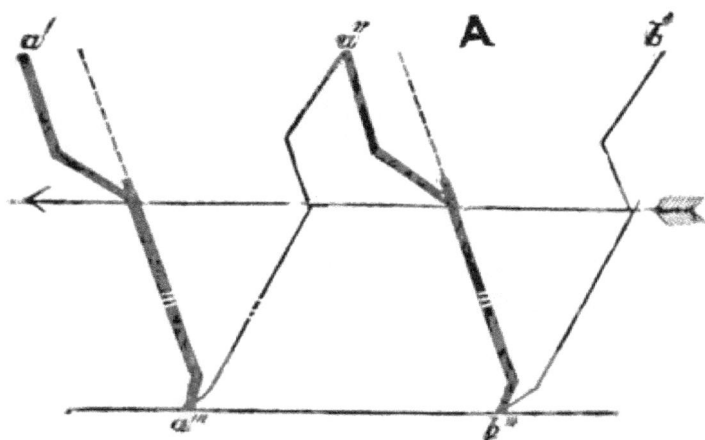

we saw that this movement was a wriggle, and we also saw that it was moved by muscles from without itself, or extrinsic muscles. So it is with the limbs, they can flex and extend themselves, but they require muscles which have their fixed points elsewhere to move them bodily onwards. Now, referring to Fig. 9, B, we find the limb flexed as represented by the right hand figure.

After being so flexed, were it not to be dragged forward by a muscle from without, but simply to again extend itself instead of alighting at a''' it would drop somewhere on the line between a''' and b'''. In order to be carried from the flexed position to the position a'' a''', *we find a long, tape-shaped muscle moves it forward through the distance we have named*, and that this muscle has *the bones of the neck and top of the head for a fixed point or fulcrum*. This is a very important point for you to remember. A fulcrum must be a fixed point, therefore when this muscle is acting, the neck must be fixed because this muscle has most extensive origin from it. Its name is 'Levator Humeri,' or in English, lifter of the arm. This is a misnomer, because the muscle does not lift the arm, but lifts the whole shoulder bodily upwards and forwards *according as the neck is situated*. This 'levator humeri' arises from the vertex of the head and from the foremost *four* bones of the neck, also through a strong elastic medium it arises from the elastic ligament of the neck. After this extensive origin, it gets a most extensive insertion to the *shoulder* as follows; the spine of the scapula or shoulder blade, the point of the shoulder, the strong outer ridge at the top of the arm bone and to the arm bone at another point near its lower end.

As the free and extensive movement of the shoulder mainly depends upon this muscle, and the longer the belly of a muscle the greater the muscle's capability for contraction, and further, as this muscle is co-extensive with the neck, it follows that *the longer the neck the more extensive the shoulder movement.* Again, as this muscle is attached to and runs parallel with the bones of the neck, and its fibres are also parallel with the bones of the neck, it follows that *the shoulder will be dragged bodily along the line of the bones of the neck.* Therefore, a horse having his head well up will necessarily lift his *shoulders* bodily upwards and forwards, whilst he will only drag his shoulder forwards whilst

Figure 9.

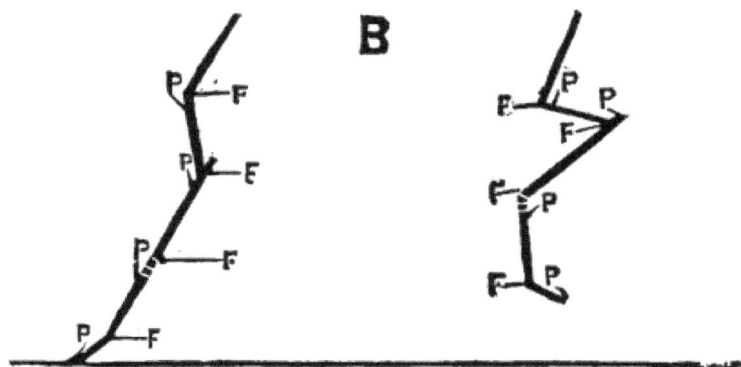

galloping with his neck and head nearer to the ground.

Never forget that the shoulder *is always dragged bodily in the line of the neck.* For high action then the first requisite is that the head and neck be held well up or the shoulder will not be lifted well up, and so forth.

57.—Flexion and extension take place by means of the muscles belonging to the limb and not from muscles having their origin else-

where. By referring to Fig. 9, *B*, we see a
fore limb in *extension*, and see also that all the
powers (P) are applied *in front* of the limb.   In
flexion we see Fig. 9, *B*, that all the powers are
applied at the *back* of the limb.   Looking at
either of these figures we see that in every case
the *power* is placed very much nearer to the *fulcrum* than the *weight*, the weight in each case
may be regarded as all the parts beneath its
respective fulcrum, so that it is evident that
speed is gained at very extensive sacrifice of
power.   In all horses' limbs, no matter what
their length and strength, there is always this
relation of power to fulcrum, so that in all
horses' limbs extent of movement or speed is
provided for more than power.

58.—The shoulder blade has two distinct movements.   We have seen that it is dragged forward
by the levator humeri muscle.   Its most extensive movement is that of its lower end, which
gives to the whole blade a pendulum movement.
Both these movements are effected by this muscle for the most part.

59.—The arm bone has also two movements.
It is dragged backwards and forwards by the
levator humeri muscle.   Its greatest movement,
however, is a pump-handle movement, having
its fulcrum or fixed point at the shoulder point.

60.—It will be seen on reference to Fig. 9, *C*, 1,
2, that we have two fore limbs in flexion.   The
figures are alike, but placed at different obliquities.   On comparing the two it will be seen that
with the same amount of flexion the 'action'

will be high or low *according to the angle formed by the body with the scapula or the limb's most fixed part*. By further comparing 1 and 2 it will be seen that 1 looks upwards and forwards, but that 2 looks forwards only. There is just one other point we must be clear upon, and that is the relation of the long axis of the fore limb to the long axis of the body. Let us agree in regarding the long axis of the fore limb at the normal when the horse is standing straight on both fore limbs, which must be perpendicular when on

Figure 9.

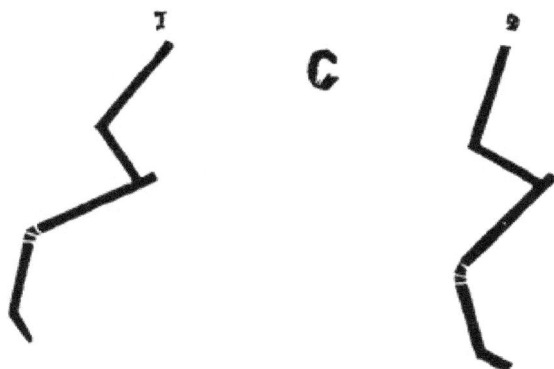

level ground. It will now be seen that the long axis of the fore limb is not necessarily at right angles with the long axis of the body. We have divided horses into three classes, and adhering to this division we find on referring to Fig. 10, that the angle formed by the long axes before referred to in the two fleet horses, 'Fisherman' and 'Saunterer,' are greater than a right angle, thus enabling the horse to 'cover more ground,' as horsemen term it. But on reference to the diagram of the Clydesdale horse, it will be seen that the two axes are at right angles. I have chosen the three from that most excellent work on the horse by Mr. Walsh (Stonehenge). In the greatest speed the long axes of the body is of necessity tilted downwards and forwards. In the heaviest draught the weight has to be thrown forwards into the collar, and the long axis of the body also thrown slightly downwards and forwards; but very much less so than in the former case. Where high 'park' action takes place, the long axis of the body must be upwards and forwards. These things being so, it follows that for either speed or action, or both, the fore limb must be placed bodily well forward, and have its long axis well in advance at its base. The horse is then said 'to cover plenty of ground.' This necessitates, as we have seen, plenty of obliquity of the shoulder blade, or in other words, the top of the blade must be well back and the shoulder point well forward. In heavy draught, the centre of gravity must be thrown well in front of the fore limbs, and kept in this relation to the rest of the body, and the long axis of the limb throughout looks downwards and forwards, and its extension forward at the base never gets beyond the perpendicular.

Figure 10.

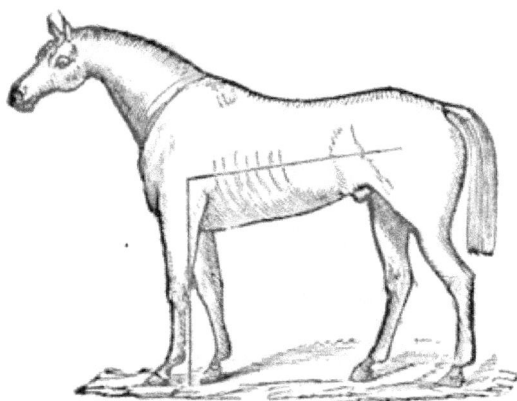

'Fisherman.'

'Saunterer.'

Clydesdale Horse.

LESSON VII.

THE FORE LIMBS.

Having come to some general conclusions regarding the fore extremity, it will be easy for us now to go quickly over a consideration of each part separately.

61.—The shoulder blade must in all classes of horses be of good length and breadth to afford space for the attachment of the many powerful muscles which take their origin from it. In the race horse it must be placed very obliquely, in order that the great length of arm required can be placed sufficiently downwards and forward, so as not to interfere with the saddle girth. The arm bone, and consequently the arm must be longer than in any other class of horse, and the angle between it and the scapula also be very great. The fore-arm also of the race horse must be long. These conditions necessitate that the 'knee' of the racer be *very near the ground,* and as the pasterns must be duly long, and, when walking, be rather upright, in order that the weight of the body in fast galloping may not unduly bend them, it follows that all this length of parts is at the expense of the metacarpal bones, which must be proportionately shorter than in any other class of horse. Indeed, the metacarpal bone cannot be too short and stout in the race horse.

62.—For draught horses the shoulder blade has need of being extremely *broad*, and placed more upright, in order to fill the upper half of the collar well when the body is thrown forward. The arm bone must be also short and stout, and at a less angle with the scapula. These conditions will enable the arm to be placed further back, and the fore legs generally to be placed *well under* the body, if possible, a little behind the perpendicular. The remaining long bones of the limb from the elbow downwards cannot be too short and thick in order that the horse may be on short, powerful legs. The fore-arm and the shins thus appear of nearly equal length.

63.—The third class, of which the hunter is a type, must have a lengthy scapula, of good breadth, and set well back. The arm must be in length longer than in the draught horse, but not so long as in the race horse. It also must be placed at an angle with the shoulder blade greater than the cart horse, but less than in the race horse. The fore-arm must be of medium length, also the shin.

64.—The knee in all classes must be very large, that is, very *deep* and *very broad from side to side*, in order that it may be well provided with buffer material as described in paragraph 11. It must not be narrow from before backwards at its *lower* part, or the horse will be what is known as 'tied in at the knee.'

65.—All the bones above the knee being clothed with muscle, we have to see that these are large and in good tone. By referring to Fig. 8, *E*, we see at a glance what the form of the parts must take in perfect development. From the knee downwards, however, we have for the most part bone not so clothed, but clearly defined in outline. The metacarpal must be stout in all cases; very broad from side to side, and of good size from behind forwards. The powerful tendons at the back of it must also have the same general outline as the bone in front of them, and they must stand out in clear relief from the bone. The outlines of the bone and tendon cannot be too distinct. The suspensary ligament, which is an unyielding structure attached to the back of the metacarpal bone and again to the back and sides of the phalanges and so slings the fetlock joint, is well seen between the metacarpal bone and the tendon, and can be felt in its lower third above the fetlock joint.

66.—The pasterns must be broad and massive. They must have plenty of length in the race horse, and be rather upright when the horse is standing, or only walking, in order that the fetlock joint may *yield well* in the gallop, and in doing so may not come too near the ground.

In draught horses they must be less upright, and they must be short and very stout.

67.—The feet of all horses must have the same general characters. The fore feet must be somewhat oval with their long axes from side to side; the hind feet too must be somewhat oval, but

their long axes is from behind forward. The wall
of the foot in front must be in a line with the
front outline of the pastern when the horse is
standing. The line formed at the top of the foot
where the hair and hoof meet must be *nearly* at
a right angle with the front line of the foot and
pastern, so that the heels will neither be too high
and the foot 'boxy' nor too low, and thereby
tender. The sole of the foot must be well *arched*,
and the frog large, wedge shaped and unbroken
or ragged. The foot must also have a bright,
shining gloss upon it, like our own nails. Shoe-
ing-smiths ought not to be allowed to remove
more of this bright substance than they can help
at the time they are rasping the turned ends of
the nails, with which they fasten on the shoe, as
it is this glue-like substance which keeps the
fibres of the hoof from splitting. They ought
never to be allowed to pare the sole of the foot
and so weaken the arch on which the column of
bones rests. After duly warning the shoeing-
smith against the infringement of these rules,
horse owners should instantly dispense with the
services of one who abuses the rasp and drawing
knife. In order to detect abuse of the rasp,
horse owners should forbid the smith to put
grease upon the hoof, and so gloss over the
injury he has inflicted with the rasp. Grease
or hoof ointment may be put on after due in-
spection has been made of the parts.

68.—The fore limbs should be set on, so that
when the horse is standing the limb may neither
be turned in nor out. *The breadth of the shoul-*

ders as seen from the front will vary according
to their muscularity, but *much more* according to
their *relative position with the trunk.* This depends upon the chest being cone-shaped. The
chest of the horse is somewhat cone-shaped with
the apex of the cone pointing forwards, and the
base pointing backwards. It is evident that the
further the shoulders are from the point of the
cone the further will they be apart from each
other. The fore legs of the horse are sometimes
said to appear 'to come out of one hole.' They
may, as we have seen, be quite as muscular as
shoulders set wider apart. Width of shoulders is
desirable for collar work, so that the fore legs
have need of being placed wider apart. We shall
say little of 'action' because that is involved in
the more general consideration of the limbs; but
we must remark that when the foot is lifted in
flexion, the lower part of the limb should be also
straight with the long axis of the body when
viewed either to the front or rear. The foot
turned out when lifted and flexed is said 'to
dish.'

The fore limb of the racer does not *necessitate*
close action, or as it is termed, 'daisy cutting'
action. Flexion is very limited, not on account
of the limb being so formed as to preclude it, but
the animal has so seldom occasion to lift his feet,
on account of being nearly always on level, unbroken ground, that habit and conservation of
energy alike tend to close stilty action. With
horses used for speed and power, which, as we
have seen, includes most horses having to go over

mixed ground, higher action becomes habitual, and in going fast on uneven ground they must habitually lift their feet well, and keep them well in advance of the body, or they must stumble and fall. Draught horses too go over all kinds of ground, and get into the habit of lifting their feet well from the ground, but in their case slower speed gives them time to rectify a false step that would bring the subject of quicker movement to the ground. Then their limbs are placed more under the body, and, being shorter, the action takes place *under* the body and not in front of it.

THE TRUNK.

69.—We must now pass in review the trunk of the horse, by which we mean the 'chest' and 'belly.'

70.—The chest, as has been before observed, is cone-shaped, having the apex of the cone pointing forward and its base backwards. This cone shape is very effectually hidden from our view in the living horse by those large muscular and bony masses, the shoulders, being placed by the side of the apex of the cone and extending backwards. The cone is made up of bones, having the backbone and upper end of the ribs for a roof, the ribs for sides and the breast bone for the floor. This bony framework contains those vital organs, the heart and lungs. In animals used for speed and power the chest must be very large, because speed and power expend much oxygen, which the lungs have to procure for the

blood from the atmosphere. As the blood feeds
upon oxygen and consumes more when the body
is in active movement, it is necessary that the
heart be large and strong to receive and send the
blood in large quantities to its airing or feeding
ground, the lungs; also that the lungs be large to
receive both it, also the air from without, which
has to meet the blood and deliver up most of its
oxygen to the blood, and in return receive impuri-
ties from the blood and carry them from the
lungs. Besides being large and strong, the heart
and lungs have to submit to quickened rhythmi-
cal movement during the exercise of speed and
power, therefore we have to see that the walls of
the chest, which we saw were formed by the
ribs, are freely *moveable*.

71.—The belly contains the organs for the con-
version of food into the substantial elements for
repair of the waste of tissue which the body is
always undergoing, but which goes on more
quickly when the animal is in greater activity.
These organs are for the most part, the stomach
and intestines with the largest gland of the body,
namely, the liver. The stomach of the horse is
comparatively small, but the intestines are very
large, and are of necessity *kept distended by residual gas*, which it is one of the functions of the
healthy body to keep *evenly balanced* in regard
both to quantity and quality. This constant dis-
tension of the intestines by healthy gas causes
that roundness and tension of the belly we see so
well marked. When the horse is in hard condition, there is a minimum quantity of healthy

gas in the bowels. This can only be when he is living on highly nutritious diet in a concentrated form, such as oats and hay. Should an animal, as in summer, be living on less nutritious diet, and this engulphed in coarse, watery, non-nutritive material, causing the digestive apparatus much work, then this residual gas is for the time greatly increased, whilst the powers are taxed to their utmost, and it not unfrequently happens that these fail in balancing the quantity of this gas, and so 'windy colic' results. It is then for us to ask first of all what the horse we are purchasing is living upon. If it is green food, we expect to find a larger belly than when living upon harder and more concentrated food. When the gas in the bowels is much less than common, it gives to the animal an unsightly appearance, and he is said to be 'tucked up in his flanks;' but I must caution you here against being deceived in the import of this. If a horse is pained in moving his hind legs, he will be tucked up in the flanks on the side on which the lame leg is, and tucked up on both flanks, of course, if lame on both hind legs. In this case, the gas in the bowels may not be proportionately less, unless he is otherwise in bad health, but it is more compressed and pushed forwards, and encroaches upon his breathing area. Some horses have habitually an appearance of less residual gas in their bowels even when in health. This gives their belly an unsightly, tucked up appearance, but it is not in itself a blemish. It will occur from overwork, and is one of the best indications we can have to stop off work, or moderate it; because, as we have reason to know, this gas must be present in sufficient quantity to maintain the digestive apparatus, so that it is merely pressed out of its legitimate area by the overworked abdominal muscles, and presses upon the heart and lungs, which causes these organs to work under undue pressure from the rear, and which will almost invariably end in inflammation (pleurisy) of their serous covering, called the pleura, if not stopped; because the pleura invests the lungs, and turns again upon itself and lines the ribs, and during breathing the two pleuras have to rub over each other, and if the lungs are unduly pressed upon from behind this friction increases and leads to inflammation.

72.—The trunk at the top has the back bone running its whole length, and we saw that each bone of the back had a bone sticking up called its spine. We further saw that it was the great length of these spines in the fore part of the back which mainly constituted the withers. The spines of the back are not all the same length, but require to be long, in order that the horse may have a strong back. The ribs must be long, so as to give depth to the chest, and they must be well rounded, otherwise the horse will be what is termed flatsided. This condition limits the extension of the lungs from side to side, so they have to extend backwards and encroach upon the alimentary organs, more especially the stomach, and this renders the animal less strong than he otherwise would be.

73.—The bottom of the chest at the girth place and between the fore legs is clothed by the very large 'pectoral' muscles, which in horses used for great speed are very highly developed, so as to give this part a very deep appearance. When these muscles are large and the withers high, the fore part of the trunk is very deep.

On referring to the horses depicted in Fig. 10, which represents our two extremes—speed and strength—it will be seen that in horses used for speed the chest is very large, and with the large powerful muscles gives the fore hand its massive appearance; while the belly is very small indeed. This gives to the trunk its *downwards and forwards axis*, as seen by our line. The draught horse, on the other hand, has, if anything, the chest smaller than the belly, so that there the two cavities are more of a size, hence the almost horizontal axis of the trunk.

LESSON VIII.

THE HIND EXTREMITIES.

Named from above downwards the bones of the hind extremities are:

The Innominate Bones.
    Femur.
Patellas.
    Tibia.
    Fibula.
    Tarsal Bones.
    Metatarsal Bones.
          Two Sessamoids.
    Suffraginal Bone.
    Coronal Bone.
      Navicular Bone.
    Pedal or Coffin Bone.

74.—The 'innominate,' or nameless bone, is so called on account of its being like nothing but itself to which anatomists can compare it. It is scientifically termed the 'pelvic girdle.' The word *pelvis* means a basin, and, save in mankind with his upright trunk, scarcely applicable to the lower animals, seeing that it is neither shaped like a basin nor properly acts as such in them. A very small portion of it, called the true pelvis, assumes more of the character and functions of a basin, and holds and protects the bladder, unimpregnated womb, &c.

This bone, in forming the foundation of what are called the 'hind quarters,' must be *thoroughly mastered* in all its aspects here pointed out.

The bone is made up of two *symmetrical* halves,* each half being made up of three distinct bones which become inseparably united in adult life at their lower middle portion. These

Figure 11.

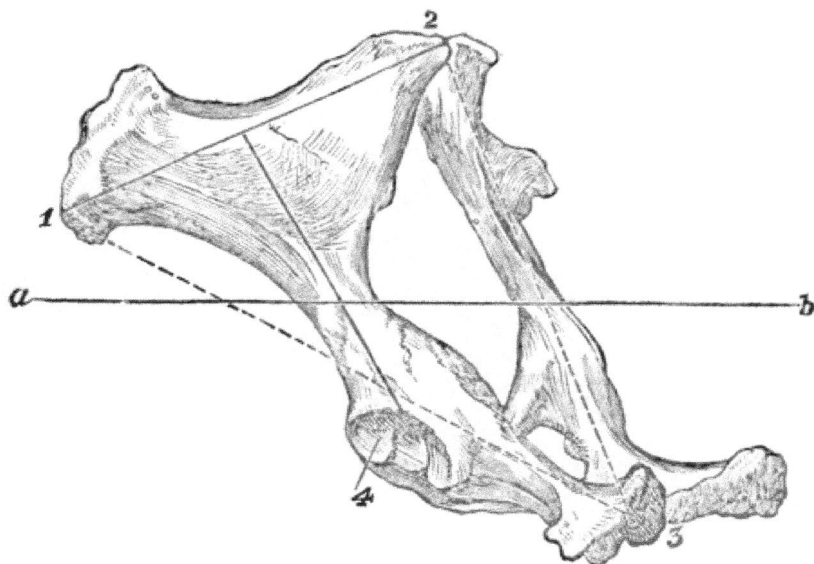

are called 'ilium,' 'ischium,' 'pubis.' We find the 'ilium' making up by far the largest part of the bone, and is all the part in front of the joint, and on which we have placed the **T** shaped figure. It also helps to form a part of the cavity of the joint. The 'ischium' is all the part behind the joint from 4 to 3. It also helps to form the joint. The 'pubis' is not well seen in our figure,

* Our description applies to either half.

but is a small flat part which with its fellow
unites the two halves of the bones together.   It
concerns us here so little that we shall not further notice it.

75.—The 'ilium' is irregularly T shaped.   The
two ends of the *top* of the T are rough and
prominent, the external end at 1 more especially
so, and is that 'point' in Mark Twain's horse
which he hired in the Sandwich Islands, situated
behind the saddle on which he hung his hat.
The other end of the T at 2 is also rough, but not
nearly so prominent, yet it too is conspicuous in
some horses.   The *top* of the T is flat and very
broad and concave from one end of the top of
the T to the other.   As it approaches the joint it
becomes narrow and nearly round like a long
bone, and like a long bone widens out to help to
form the joint.

76.—The 'ischium' part of bone (between 4 and
3) is seen to be quite like a long bone in its centre in being round and narrow, and widens out in
front to help to form the joint, and also widens
out behind, and forms a large, rough prominence,
3, we see by the side of the root of the tail.

77.—The 'ilium' and 'ischium' being practi-
cally all one bone, we will refer to them as such,
and call the *united structure* the '*ilio-ischium*.'
The ilio-ischium plays the most important part in
the formation of the hind quarters as we shall
see.   We have seen that it has three points all
large and rough, and which give origin to large
muscles.   Now we find these points extremely
useful, indeed *indispensable landmarks* in judg-

ing the hind quarters. If point 1 be placed high up on a level with point 2, it gives the hips a rugged, coarse appearance, as in Fig. 12, the large, rugged point being all the more conspicuous. Then again, if point 3 be placed very low down, it gives the quarters a drooping appearance, therefore we have to regard the relations of these three points to *two axes*, one axis is the long axis of the body generally, and may be represented by the line *a b*, which we shall call the axis of the *antero-posterior obliquity;* the other axis is represented by the dotted line between points 2 and 3, which we shall call the axis of the *lateral obliquity.*

Seeing that point 2 is fixed always, being bound down by unyielding ligaments to the solid portion of the back bone, called the *sacrum,* and the sacrum is, as we have seen, a part of, and a continuation of the back bone, it follows that when this *ilio-ischium* alters its relation to the line *a b* (axis of antero-posterior obliquity) it is the point 3 which is affected and lifted up so as to form straight quarters as in the Arab; drooping quarters as in the cob and trotting horse, or a medium as in the hunter class.

Again, when the lateral obliquity is affected we may regard the points 2 and 3 as being fixed, or what is better, regard the dotted line 2 3 as a door post on which the bone *ilio-ischium* is swung, then it is evident that it is the point 1, and with it the joint 4, that is affected, the former most so, and we get the *level ragged hips* well seen in the 'bus horse, where the point 1 is

on a level with point 2, and where the widest
part of the quarters is at the top (Fig. 12), or we
have point 1 much lowered as in Fig. 13, seen in
the higher breeds, where the breadth of the quarters is much lower down.   Notice, of course, that

Figure 12.   Figure 13.

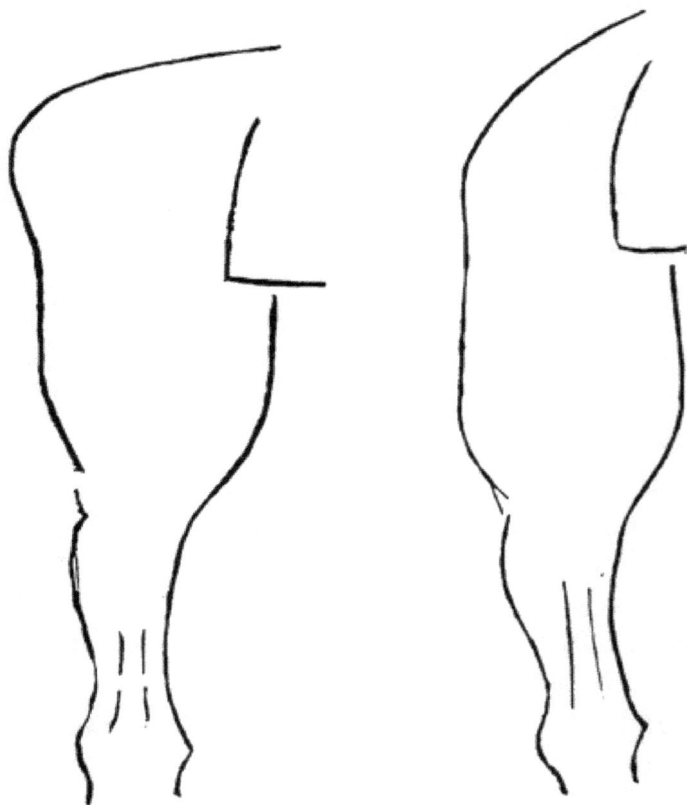

as it is point 1 which determines the breadth of
the quarters in all cases, the quarters will be
widest at the top or lower down according to the
relative position of point 1, to the axis of the
. lateral obliquity (dotted line 2, 3).

The hip joint is *largely affected* by both obliquities. It will be highest in straight quarters, and lowest in drooping quarters. The length of the thigh bone is the same in all positions of the joint so that the stifle joint will be lowest and furthest advanced under the body in drooping quarters. This condition is most favorable for fast walking and trotting, but little favorable for galloping, because the more the quarters droop, the more is the femur or thigh bone directed forwards and downwards, and having a limited motion, and placed almost at right angles with the ilio-ischium, its movement backwards is therefore less, and incapable of being stretched well back in the gallop. The femur is placed at right angles, or nearly so, with the ilio-ischium, so that its arc of motion will be the further advanced the more drooping the quarters.

To judge the length of the femur in the living horse, you draw an imaginary line from the prominence at the tail to point 1, then the head or top of the femur is at the end of the first third of this distance, and the other end is quite well represented by the depression or notch, formed at the stifle joint. The femur is a very thick bone, and very powerful, and clothed by the large muscles of the thigh. It extends from the socket on the ilio-ischium, whilst the lower end is placed upon the two bones below (tibia and fibula) with the patella or knee-cap in front, and thus forms the *largest* joint in the body, called the stifle joint (our knee joint).

78.—One bone only, the tibia, reaches from the

stifle joint to the hock joint (See Fig. 14).   It is a
long bone with two ends.   The upper end as
aforesaid helps to form the stifle joint, and is
rather a large end.   The lower end is *small*, and

Figure 14.

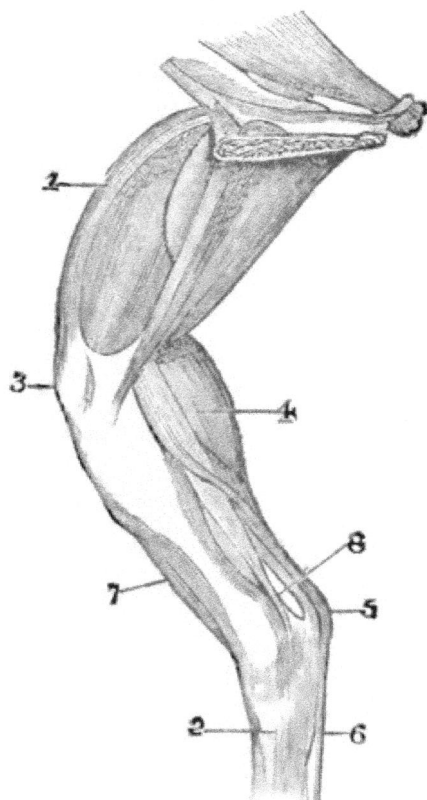

1. The large muscles of the thigh.
2. The lower part of the hock at the usual seat of spavin.
3. The patella, or "knee-cap;" immediately below this the depression is over the joint.
4. Muscles at the back of the tibia, corresponding to the "calf"
of our leg.
5. Point of hock.
6. Curb place.
7. Bellies of muscles on outer aspect of leg.
8. Space, the seat of "thoro-pin."

with the astragalus forms the true hock joint. The length or shaft of the bone is not round, but *has three flat sides;* one side looking backwards having upon it the bellies of large muscles corresponding to the *calf* of our own leg. Another surface looks inwards and forwards, and is covered by skin only, as seen in Fig. 14, just as in ourselves, and in us is called the shin, and can be felt as a bony-surface from our stifle or knee down to our hock or ankle, where it ends in a *very sharp bony point* in both cases called the *inner maleolus.*

You should make an effort to remember this prominent bony point called the *inner maleolus,* because it forms a prominent land-mark in describing the hock. The remaining side of this bone looks outwards and forwards, and is covered by powerful muscles, Fig. 14, 7, which if you grasp your right leg with your right hand in front, half way between the knee and ankle, and then raise your toes without moving your foot or leg, you will feel to contract. This outer surface then is covered by the bellies of the muscles which lift the toes upwards, and in the horse lifts his foot forward.

We have, in our remarks, spoken of an *inner maleolus,* implying the existence of an outer maleolus. The outer maleolus is formed by the lower end of the 'fibula' in ourselves, but in the horse the 'fibula' is only rudimentary, and does not reach down to the hock, or ankle, but is merely a spicula of bone having no function or use whatever.

79.—The hock* (our ankle) is a highly important joint on account of the frequency of its break-downs. It is placed *under*, and forms an *angle* with the large bone, the tibia, which transmits the weight of the body on its upper surface, and is placed over, and is in a *line* with the long bone below, the metatarsal bone, which has to meet the weight of the body at this point, and form a support for it every time the body has to be propelled forward. We must never lose sight of the fact that *the angle is at the bottom of the tibia*, and at the *top* of the hock, and that the direction of the weight of the body is represented by the long axis of the tibia. This direction of weight is easiest combated the less the angle formed at the hock, just as a straight upright pillar will bear a greater weight than one which has a bend or angle in it, and the greater this bend or angle, the less able is the pillar to support weight put upon it. The weight of the horse is, we have said, transmitted through the tibia, and is not a *dead* weight so to speak, that is to say it is not like the steady downward pressure of a weight having no other influences save gravity on the one hand and the resisting medium on which it rests on the other. It may be compared to the pressure exerted on the end of the village urchin's bow when he has planted one end on the ground, is bending the wood with his right knee whilst he holds the bow firmly pressed to

---

* The student should procure the bones of a sound hock. Any horse-slaughterer's man will procure and prepare these for a shilling or so.

the ground with his left hand, and is dragging
the string upwards to the notch or catch with his
right hand. In such a case the end resting on the
ground is pressed downwards with the left hand,
and is dragged upwards through the medium of
the string with the other. Such a weight differs
much from a so-called dead weight. Excluding
the long bones above and below which meet the
hock, and regarding only the intrinsic bones of
hock, we can divide them into three sets according to their functions; namely—

1. The gliding bone.
2. The lever bone.
3. The buffer bones.

The gliding bone is called the astragalus, and is
a large cubical block which carries the two *large*
gliding surfaces, on which glides the *small* end of
the tibia. These two large gliding surfaces have
a screw-like form which causes the parts below
the hock, when the toe is lifted, to move outwards. Then again, this gliding surface is almost
parallel with the long axis of the hock and parts
below. Then again, and this is very important to
remember, when the foot is on the ground, the
leg at its straightest, and the very *small* end of
the tibia resting upon the *top* of this large gliding
surface, the hock appears large, but when the leg
is lifted, and the *small* end of the tibia slides
necessarily to the bottom of this large gliding
surface, the hock *looks small*, therefore it is the
relation of this large gliding surface to the *small*
surface at the lower end of the tibia which deter-

mines the apparent size of the hock. *It follows that a bent hock which appears smaller may be as large as a straight hock which appears larger.*

The lever bone, or 'calcaneum,' is placed at the top of the hock at the back, and is a lever of the second order. The end of the long arm of this lever is called the point of the hock, and corresponds with our heel. It has attached to it the tendon (called 'Tendo Achilles') of the large muscle whose belly forms the so-called calf of our leg. All depends upon the length of this lever whether the 'calves' are large or small, because the longer this long arm, the less will be the strength required to work it. Negroes have small calves to their legs very often, because their heels are so long. A well-bred European with his short large, muscle to *work* it, and so can boast of 'having a good leg.' The 'calf' of the horse is very much concealed on account of the large muscles of the back of the thigh being inserted into the back and upper third of the tibia surrounding the 'calf' to some extent. The muscles on the outer side of the tibia (Fig. 14, 7) called the *gaskin* muscles, well seen in Fig. 15, are extremely prominent, and measurable with the eye, and, as we have seen, extend the toe and foot. Little notice then need be taken of the long arm of the lever under consideration. With a long lever arm, and the same bulk and strength of 'calf' required for a short lever arm attached to it, the hock would be torn asunder. This, as we have seen, cannot be the case. The weight surface of the lever is applied against the astraga-

lus. The fulcrum concerns us most, as it is fixed
by means of ligaments which are sometimes torn
or otherwise injured, and which swell and in-
flame in consequence, and the horse is then said

Figure 15.

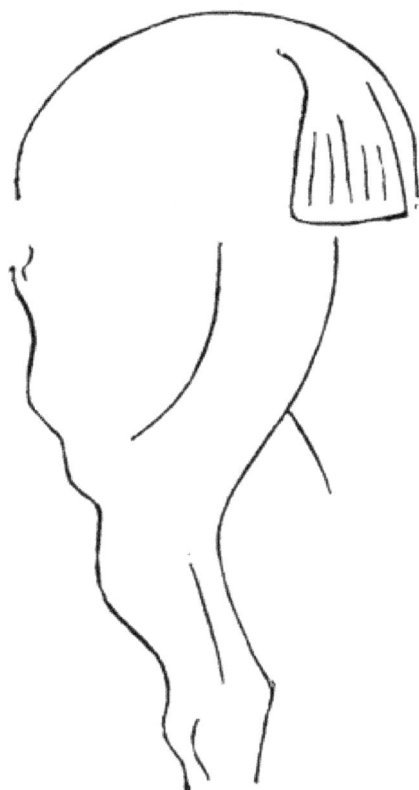

to have 'sprung a curb.' The place of this occur-
rence is marked at Fig. 14, 6.

The 'irregular' bones or buffers are placed at
the lower part of the hock, and are two tiers having joints between them. They are very much
jarred when the hock is flexed smartly as in that
quick fascinating hock action we sometimes wit-

ness, and then the inner ones undergo change and throw out a soft plastic material which in time hardens into bone, and is called 'bone spavin' or a 'jack.' Much depends on the size of these buffer bones. If they are large they serve their purpose, and we may have a good hock. They form the whole of the lower part of the hock, so that we must look for this part to be large in every way.

80.—The bone below the hock is called the metatarsal bone, and is like the metacarpal bone of the fore leg, only it must be thickest from before backwards.

81.—The remaining bones are for the most part like those of the fore leg.

LESSON IX.

HIND EXTREMITIES—CONTINUED.

The hind extremities are the *propellers* of the body, and the fore extremities are the weight bearers, roughly speaking. The same general remarks which were made regarding the fore extremities apply equally to the hind ones. The ilio-ischium representing the scapula, &c. Where we find the bellies of groups of muscles, there we find bulk and rotundity. Those who have an eye for the beauty of curves will find pleasing curved lines in the outlines of a horse in condition. The absence of these beautiful curves is well marked in horses not in condition. For example, standing at the side, but a little behind a hunter in condition (see Fig. 15), we see prominently among other curved lines the most beautiful curves formed by the outlines of the muscles of the hind-quarters and leg; indeed to all, whether judges or lovers of horseflesh or not, this profusion of elegant and varying curves set forth on a shining coat, grace of movement and the fire of excess of life, gives a thrill of pleasure which possibly no object in nature can surpass. These beauties are not surpassed by the most perfect female (human) figure, and seeing that in our

social life these latter are hidden, undoubtedly a
hunter in highest condition, prepared for the
chase, is perhaps the most entrancing of sights.
Look out then in judging a horse for beautiful

Figure 16.

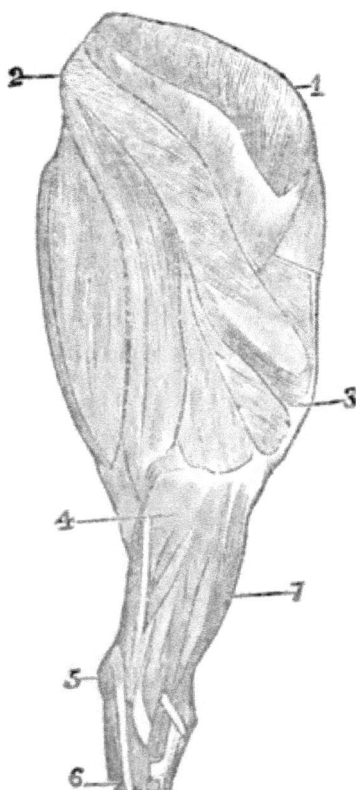

1. Outer point of ilium.	5. Point of hock.
2. Point of ischium.	6. Curb place.
3. Stifle joint.	7. Gaskins.
4. Calf of leg.	

curves. There are some—but they must be first
rate judges—who can afford to lose sight of these
curves in purchasing what they term a poor horse,

i.e., a horse not in condition. When this is so, they must see to the *relative length and bulk* of the levers (bones) being what is desirable, also that the joints are *large* and *flat*, and of course an absence of blemishes. If the bones of the extremities are of proper length and stoutness, then —except of course in disease—the muscles will either be in good condition, or will be capable of being made so, and they will be massive and present bold, beautiful curved outlines.

The ilio-ischium should be broad so as to present abundant surface for muscular attachment. If the **T** shaped upper surface looks upwards from the quarters being 'ragged' from point 1 (Fig. 11), being on a level with point 2, then the body of muscles occupying this space will present a curve with a convexity looking directly upwards (see Fig. 12). But should point 1 be much lower, the convexity of the curve looks outwards and upwards (see Fig. 13), and the curve formed —as seen when standing behind—in the latter case between point 1 and the stifle joint will be less broken, and therefore the more elegant. The depth of the thigh is well seen from behind, but it appears deeper, if not really so, in such as have straight quarters, for reasons we have before seen. There is just one other obliquity of the innominate bone which we have as yet not mentioned. It obtains between the two symmetrical halves of the innominate bone—in other words, between the two ilio-ischia bones. When these bones are much divergent in front and their after points converge, a very defective 'setting on' of the hind limbs results and the hind limbs look outwards. This being so, the hocks are closer together, and the horse is said to be 'cow hocked.' The ilio-ischia bones ought to be as parallal as possible, so that the hind limbs look straight forwards and backwards, when the horse is standing. In moving, the hip joint and the screw-like astragalus cause the limb naturally to assume the slightly outward aspect. In ourselves this is so, and the dancing master or drill sergeant is not to be thanked that our toes are a little out-turned, because as the hip joint is constituted they could not be otherwise.

It is hoped that the above remarks will form a good guide to those who are desirous of *thinking out* for themselves the numberless points to be observed in horse judging.

We shall now close these remarks with a few observations on the hock.

THE HOCK.

82.—Of all the joints in the body this is the most important. We must refer the reader to our description of the bones in Lesson VIII., and remind him that according to the size of the individual bones alone the *apparent* size of the hock does not depend, but more upon the angle at which the tibia impinges upon the astragalus. This is well seen in extreme flexion, when the hock seems to disappear, leaving nothing but its so-called point in view. The lower fourth or more of the hock is made up of the buffer bones

in front and at the sides, consequently it is these
which give the lower part of the hock size. They
must be large but not necessarily coarse, but they
may be large and coarse and of unequal size in
the two hocks and yet be quite healthy and free
from 'spavin.' The top of the metatarsal bone
on which they mainly rest must also be large.
When this latter is small we have a grave defect;
but when it is not only small, but forms with the
buffer bones of the hock an angle, we have a very
grave defect called 'curby hocks.'

The hock should present on its inner surface a
big, flat, square appearance, and when a horse-
man speaks of liking a big, flat, square hock, he
refers to the inner aspect of the hock. The
boundaries of this so-called square are as follows:
the internal maleolus or lowest inner point of the
tibia; the extreme point of the hock; the front
part of the head of the tibia; lastly, the head of
the small inner metatarsal bone. These points
form the four points of the square, and the sides
are the imaginary lines between these four points.
It is not within the scope of this work to speak
of morbid conditions—such as spavin, curb, ring-
bone, splint, and so forth, but we must caution the
reader against an appearance of 'curb.' When
the head of the outer small metatarsal bone is
large, it gives the side aspect of the really good
well-made hock a 'curbed' appearance, because
the line from the extreme point of hock to the
fetlock at the back should be *quite straight*, and
is straight in all except badly formed hocks and
such as have 'curbs.' Even when the head of

the outer small bone named is large and breaks this line when viewed from the side, the straight line is still found when you approach the hock and run your fingers down the middle line of the parts behind.

The angle at the hock we saw was formed by the tibia impinging upon the astragalus, and we further saw that the less the angle the weaker the hock. The hind legs must therefore be as upright, or rather as straight as possible, in order to be as strong as possible. But we have already seen that power (strength) is universally gained at the expense of speed, which, in turn, can only be obtained by quickness and extent of motion of the parts most concerned in speed, so that straight hind limbs are stronger, but have less of that quick perfect flexion or hock action which has such an attractive appearance.

The front and back of the hock must also have plenty of breadth. The point of the hock short of being ' capped ' cannot be too broad.

83.—The metatarsal bone must be short and stout, and the hock as near the ground as possible. This bone is thickest from before backwards, and as the back tendon must have the same characters as we described in the case of the like structure in the fore limb, it follows that these parts will be altogether deeper from before backwards. As in the case of the fore limb, the tendon must stand out distinctly from the bone, and the suspensory ligament must also be well defined.

84.—The pasterns must also have much the

same qualities as those of the fore limb in each class of horse.

85.—The foot also must have the same general characters as the fore foot, but the long axis of its oval is always from before backwards. The hind foot does not call forth the fraction of the amount of care as is the case with the fore foot. It is less often unsound, and its unsoundness less frequently leads to the same disastrous results. It is well, however, to look to it much in the same manner as in the case of the fore foot.

LESSON X.

THE WIND, COLOR, HEIGHT, COAT AND HAIR, AGE.

The term 'wind' is used by horsemen to signify the respiration or breathing capabilities. It is not necessary to describe in detail defects in 'wind.' Normal or healthy breathing, or 'wind,' will here be described, and from that defects may be recognized.

When a healthy horse of average size is standing quietly in his stable, he breathes from eight to ten or twelve times a minute. I here use the term breathes in its popular sense, which all, I believe, understand. If the back of the hand and fingers be placed against the ribs, just behind the elbow, the heart will be felt to knock the side in beating about four times the breathing rate, so that a healthy horse having a pulse of thirty-six per minute will breathe about nine times per minute. In all cases there ought to be this ratio 1—4 or thereabout. Should this ratio be absent to any marked extent, such for instance as a breathing rate of fifteen and a pulse rate of forty, disease is present. Exercise in moderation increases both pulse and respiration, both are quickened, but the ratio is more or less retained. Anyhow, when the horse comes to stand and rest, the ratio in health is soon re-ëstablished. In very small horses, such as Shetland ponies, the pulse may be forty or forty-four per minute, and the breathing eleven, but there is still the ratio 1—4 in health. Many things disturb this ratio— disease, fright, grief, joy, &c.—by quickening the pulse, and affecting less the breathing.

In order to acquire dexterity in judging the 'wind' it is best to get a horse known to have perfect 'wind' into a grass field, and have him slowly trotted round you in a circle about the size of an ordinary horse-rider's circus. Noise must *necessarily* be made in breathing, but there ought to be no distress exhibited, no difficulty in getting breath, no noises except soft blowing—no whistling or grunting. After a reasonable time, long before the animal shows signs of distress, he should be stopped, and notice be taken *how long* the breathing is in quieting down. This time is easily judged if the examiner will judge the horse by himself—if healthy—as the same length of time is required after the same proportion of exertion in the two cases. In the autumn when the horse has on a long coat he will feel distress earlier, and congestion of the lungs will be more easily induced. If exercise be not followed by quieted respiration, some defect is present. Of course, if undue exercise has been taken, then the lungs, although healthy, may have become congested. Again, attention should be given to the movements of the ribs on either side. The ribs should expand freely on both sides. In some diseases of the lungs one may become 'deaf,' or a great part of one may be so, then the work is thrown on to the sound lung, and the breathing capabilities so much decreased. This shows itself by the affected side having more limited movement. As a general thing, fat, gross subjects have a diminished breathing capacity, therefore they are sooner distressed, and their breathing does not quiet down so soon after exertion. Pregnancy encroaches still more on the breathing capacities. Horses used to going out of a walking pace are more likely to have good breathing capacities than those used for slow work. With draught horses, pulling a load will give a better idea of breathing capabilities than any other exercise—care being taken that the collar fits well and does not bear on the windpipe.

Some strike and threaten a horse up against a wall, or while standing in his stall, with a stick. Such a proceeding does not try the 'wind,' but will in some cases elicit the peculiar grunt or roar in 'roarers,' and thus save further trial. Further than this the test is useless and misleading.

COLOR.

There is an old saying that a good horse cannot be a bad color. This, like most *sayings*, has a germ of truth in it. Were we to have a free choice, in all cases we should select our color as follows: the best color undoubtedly is dark brown, with black points; the next best color is bay, with black points. Light chestnuts are good; but dark chestnuts are objectionable, as it is notorious that after seven years old their fore feet are often contracted. Grays and whites are not bad colors. Black is a hardy color; white stockings if they exist largely on the same horse are objectionable, especially if the absence of pigment or coloring matter extends to the horn of the feet. Of all colors, yellow or Cleveland bays, piebalds, and dark red chestnuts are the most objectionable. In the choice of a horse, however, the purchaser should ask himself the question: Does the horse's color offend the eye? If not, and if the horse be otherwise desirable, the color ought not to be an obstacle.

HEIGHT.

Having regard to most speed, we should have the largest dimensions possible, and therefore the greatest height compatible with perfection in symmetry. The greatest power also requires the greatest bulk. A combination of speed and power, as exhibited in our type the hunter, has its highest expression in horses about fifteen and a half hands high; half a hand more or less being unessential.

THE SKIN AND ITS APPENDAGES.

The skin of the thoroughbred is extremely thin and delicate, and allows the veins to be seen through it, and is covered with fine hair. That of the draught horse is thick. That of the hunter, or power and speed representative, is a mean between the two extremes, and shows as clearly as most things whether the horse in question inclines to being well bred and thin skinned or the reverse.

Much mane and tail is a sign of low breeding. A slight silky mane, with or without a little wave in the hair, is a desirable thing. The same may be said of the tail.

AGE.

Horses, as a rule, are considered at their best at from five to ten years of age. Much depends on the age at which they are put to work. The author has in his mind's eye a case in which a gentleman used to break his horses at four, but did not begin to use them until eight. These horses, to the author's own knowledge, were at their prime from eight to twenty years of age.

As horses are now treated, their ages may be compared with that of man as follows:—

A horse at	5	equals a man at		20
"	10	"	"	40
"	15	"	"	50
"	20	"	"	60
"	25	"	"	65
"	30	"	"	70
"	35	"	"	90
"	40	"	"	105

This calculation supposes both subjects to be well treated.

THE END.